Katy McElroy

Eclectus Parrots

Everything About Purchase, Care,
Feeding, and Housing

Filled with Full-color Photographs
Illustrations by Michele Earle-Bridges

BARRON'S

2 CONTENTS

ECLECTUS PARROTS AS PETS

Parrots are capable of living 30 years or more in captivity. Choosing an Eclectus as a lifelong companion is a commitment that should not be taken lightly.

Do You Really Want a Parrot?

All parrots have one thing in common: They are wild creatures. Unlike domesticated dogs and cats that have been bred in captivity for thousands of years, and are genetically programmed to accept us and to live with us on *our* terms, most parrots have been breeding readily in captivity for only the last 15 years. In all probability, the parents or grandparents of the hand-fed baby parrot that you purchase today from a breeder or pet store were wild-caught, imported birds. A baby parrot born in captivity may be tame, but it is still far better equipped physically and emotionally to deal with life in the wild than with life as someone's pet. A parrot may live 30 to 60 years or more, so it is a lifetime job

Male and female Grand Eclectus (E. roratus roratus). Because of the extreme color difference between the sexes, it was once thought that male and female Eclectus were separate species.

teaching it to successfully and happily coexist with people. Someone unprepared for this kind of commitment would be better off with a more compliant companion animal.

Life with a parrot is often a challenge. Its love has to be earned and its trust is easily broken by inappropriate behavior such as neglect, carelessness, or rough handling. A parrot can be one of the most entertaining and delightful pets you will ever own, *but only if you accept, understand, and enjoy its natural characteristics*. They are noisy, messy, destructive, demanding, and at times aggressive, and many lose their homes because of the annoyance they cause less committed family members. A parrot must never be bought with the idea of it being a conversation piece or an expensive decoration. Their emotional and physical needs are too complex to make them good substitutes for paintings or potted plants.

A happy, healthy parrot will demand your attention and try your patience, but if you accept it for the wild thing it is, it will repay you with a lifetime of love and laughter.

The Eclectus Today

Books and articles about parrots written before the early 1990s often devoted much space to the discussion of taming and training wild-caught, imported birds. Prior to that time, the vast majority of parrots available to the U.S. pet trade came from wild populations. Sadly, the mortality suffered during capture, transit, and quarantine sometimes reached 80 percent. No one who has seen photographs of frightened, sick, and injured wild parrots stuffed tightly into crates will soon forget the image. Because parrots do not produce large numbers of offspring and cannot rebuild their wild populations quickly, the combination of excessive trade and habitat destruction in range countries has been devastating for some species.

Imported Eclectus parrots, though admired for their beauty, rarely lost their distrust of people and were disappointing pets. During the 1970s and '80s, most parrots were still being fed a nutritionally inadequate seed diet that proved especially damaging to Eclectus. As a result, they received a reputation for being dull, delicate, and short-lived. The Convention of International Trade in Endangered Species (CITES), an international treaty with more than 120 member nations, currently either regulates or prohibits the trade of all parrots, with the exception of budgies and cockatiels. In 1992 the U.S. government adopted the Wild Bird Conservation Act, which prohibits the commercial import of almost all wild parrots for the pet trade. As the numbers of imported birds declined, the interest in captive breeding increased and breeders found that, compared to other parrots, Eclectus reproduced readily in captivity.

All of the young Eclectus parrots now available to the U.S. pet trade are domestically bred birds. The huge difference in pet quality between wild-caught and captive-bred parrots is not surprising when one considers the emotional baggage a wild bird must shed to overcome its fear of people. Most breeders in this country remove baby Eclectus from their parents between the ages of one and three weeks to begin the process of hand-feeding. This insures that the baby grows up tame, trusting, and easy to handle. Captive breeding combined with an improved knowledge of avian nutrition has finally brought the wonderful pet qualities of the Eclectus parrot to the attention of the public. If one takes the time to seek out a reputable breeder or bird shop, it should not be difficult to find a well-socialized, healthy young bird.

Appearance

Colors

The Eclectus parrot is not only beautiful but also unique in several ways. The extreme dimorphism, or color difference between the sexes, is such that as late as the early nineteenth century the male and female were thought to be separate species. The male is basically green with bright red under the wings and extending down the sides of his breast. The bend of the wing is bright turquoise, shading to a deeper blue on the flight feathers. His bright orange and yellow beak is often described as resembling a piece of candy corn. The female has a bright red head and neck, dark red or burgundy back and wings, and, depending on her subspecies, a royal blue, lavender, or purple breast. Her beak is black. The males of the five subspecies available in this country are similar in appearance, which unfortunately has led to considerable hybridizing by inexperienced or careless breeders.

Feathers

Also unusual are the feathers of the head, neck, and breast, which have a fur or hairlike appearance. These feathers lack the interlocking barbules or tiny hooks that normally "zip" feather barbs together, giving the surface of each feather a smooth, unbroken appearance.

Natural Behaviors and Personality

We can learn much about our pet Eclectus by studying their natural behaviors. They differ from most parrots in that the female is the dominant partner. She chooses to accept or reject the male's advances, picks the nesting site, incubates the eggs, and cares for the chicks. The male guards the nest area, but once the eggs are laid, he often isn't permitted inside the nesting cavity. Once incubation has begun, the female generally leaves the nest only to stretch her wings and to be fed regurgitated food by her mate. The male continues to bring food to the hen during the entire time she is incubating eggs and caring for the helpless, naked chicks.

Though most pairs of Eclectus seem to enjoy each other's company, they do not form the tight pair bond that is seen with most other parrot species. They are very much aware of each other and constantly make eye contact, but there is little mutual touching and preening or other obvious signs of affection. The male becomes adept at reading the body language of his mate and can quickly determine if she is in a receptive mood. One sideways glance is often enough to send him scurrying to a safer perch!

This quiet awareness is one of the nicest things about the Eclectus' personality. A happy companion bird seems genuinely concerned about its owner. If you glance up at your bird, you will often find it thoughtfully gazing back. Eclectus parrots are responsive to their owner's mood and tone of voice. They enjoy interacting with the people in their lives without being overly demanding of their time and attention or needing to be in the middle of every activity.

It has been said that the Eclectus male is the better pet of the two, and that may be true to some extent because of his easygoing nature. There are a great many sweet Eclectus hens, however, whose owners would probably disagree. Though likely to be more strong-willed than the male, a female Eclectus is capable of being a gentle and charming pet.

Character Traits

Their Need for Social Interaction

In the wild an Eclectus parrot is a social creature that benefits from the safety and security of being part of a flock. Even though much of that flock interaction might consist of quarreling noisily over choice food or roosting spots, an Eclectus was never meant to live a solitary existence. A single pet bird needs to feel that it is part of its human flock and it is important to locate its cage where it can watch family activities. A well-adjusted pet Eclectus with a large cage, a moveable playstand, and lots of toys can generally cope with the absence of family members while they are at work, so long as busy schedules don't get in the way of daily one-on-one time spent with the bird. Perhaps because males and females

This male Eclectus displays the red and blue coloring under his wings as he bathes in a spray mist.

do not form strong pair bonds with one another, a pet Eclectus is less likely to develop a marked preference for one person, especially if all members of the family take turns doing things that the bird enjoys, such as sharing their food, showering with them, allowing it to sit close by while they work at the computer, or snuggle with them while they read or watch television. Anyone who lives with a cockatoo or other possessive psittacine that will settle for nothing less than its preferred person's undivided attention will appreciate the undemanding nature of Eclectus parrots.

Though Eclectus enjoy gentle handling and being included in their owner's activities, they don't usually solicit much touching and petting. They definitely don't respond well to rough play or petting that ruffles their feathers, but Eclectus that have been conditioned to light stroking and gentle snuggling when young will often continue to enjoy it throughout their lives.

Their Need for a Tranquil Environment

Eclectus parrots have an aura of quiet calm about them that can be misleading. Unlike other species of parrots that will scream, fly, or attempt to hide when frightened or upset, an Eclectus will hold perfectly still as if hoping it won't be noticed. If the stressful situation is allowed to continue, the unhappy bird may resort to feather plucking or screaming, both of which can be difficult habits to break. Over time a stressed bird is likely to develop serious health problems.

Cages with play tops are popular, but some parrots may become territorial when allowed to play on their cages.

Eclectus parrots enjoy being included in their owners' activities.

Eclectus parrots are probably happiest in adult households where there is structure and continuity in the day-to-day existence. A noisy, active household with young children is likely to be too chaotic to provide the security and stability these intelligent, sensitive birds need. That is not meant to imply that Eclectus are fragile or difficult. The author sold one young Solomon Island male that now commutes daily with his owner between her home and business. He has a playstand in her shop where he spends the day amusing himself with his toys and greeting customers, and he happily accompanies her on vacation trips. Another of the author's young parrots was bought by a couple who retired to a houseboat. This lucky fellow supervises food preparation in the galley, perfectly mimics seagulls and other water birds, weathers the storms, and obviously delights in the neverending change of scenery as they make their way between summers on the Great Lakes and winters in Florida.

Their Unsuitability as Pets for Children

When frightened, angry, or upset, even the gentlest parrot may react by biting—hard! An observant adult can usually avoid this by watching the bird's body language and learning to understand and respect its moods. Even well-meaning children, including most adolescents, are not sensitive enough to be aware of a parrot's moods and usually have no idea

when their noise or erratic behavior might be causing a bird fear or stress. For this reason, and the fact that they are happiest in a serene environment, an Eclectus is not a suitable pet for a child unless it is acquired as a family

A spacious cage and lots of toys are necessary for the health and well-being of an Eclectus parrot.

Placing the Cage

Parrots are gregarious creatures and do not thrive in solitary confinement. The cage should be placed where the bird can easily watch and be a part of family activities.

endeavor and handled with respect, gentleness, and constant adult supervision.

Getting Along with Other Pets

Though birds, dogs, and cats often enjoy and benefit from each other's company, especially when their owners are away for long periods of time, so much depends on their personalities. Introductions should be made slowly and carefully with the parrot safely caged and watched closely for signs of fear or stress. Dogs or cats should not be left alone in a room with a caged bird until they have proven themselves trustworthy over weeks or months. Most well-fed house cats are not interested in Eclectus-size birds. If a cat insists on stalking the bird, a squirt of water will usually change its mind. Dogs can become very excited when a bird is out of its cage, especially if it flaps its wings or flies. A bird may never fully recover from the physical or emotional trauma of having its cage jumped on or knocked over by a natural predator.

Many people obtain a great deal of enjoyment from watching their parrots and other pets playing peacefully together, but this sort of interaction should be closely monitored at all times. Even if a dog or cat exhibits perfect manners, a playful parrot may stalk and attempt to nip them. The saliva from dogs and cats is toxic to birds and a bite can cause a fatal septicemia with Pasteurella bacteria in 24 hours. Cats lick their paws, so even a minor scratch wound is serious and requires antibiotic treatment by a veterinarian.

Always be sure that the bird is safely caged if someone visits with a strange dog or cat. Pet ferrets, snakes, or other large reptiles, no matter how gentle, should never be trusted around a bird.

Noise

The normal vocalizations of a happy, healthy parrot can be too loud for many people. Though pet Eclectus have a reputation for being less noisy than, say, Amazon parrots or cockatoos, they are large birds that are easily capable of making themselves heard by close neighbors. Those who have been fortunate enough to observe wild Eclectus parrots in their natural habitat invariably comment on how raucous and noisy these flocks are as they squabble over food and roosting spots or fly from place to place. A busy, happy, well-cared-for pet Eclectus with a large cage and lots of toys can be one of the quietest of all parrots, although the contact calls that it makes as it attempts to stay in touch with its human flock when they leave the room can be loud. An adult male Eclectus will screech a warning when anyone approaches his nesting site, and a pet may do the same if a stranger gets too close to his cage or he observes a visitor through a window.

Noisy households invariably produce noisy parrots. Loud television programs, boisterous children, and barking dogs may inspire an Eclectus to compete with or to protest the racket. A bird that has been taught to scream may use its newly discovered skill in ways that its owners consider annoying, such as requesting food or attention. As with any habit, screaming is easier to prevent than to stop.

The contented chortling sounds that an Eclectus makes when it knows that all is right with its world are varied, pleasant, and uncommon to any other parrot.

Space Requirements

The old rule of thumb that suggested giving a bird as big a cage as it could turn around in with wings outstretched has led to more bored, unhappy, screaming, feather-plucking, neurotic parrots than any other factor. Parrots were meant to fly great distances every day, but in order to keep them as pets it is usually necessary to cage them for long periods of time. Therefore, when we take on the responsibility of a companion bird, we need to do everything that we can to make that bird's life in captivity a busy, happy one.

The *minimum* size cage for a pet Eclectus parrot is 24 inches wide by 36 inches long by about 60 inches high (61 × 91 × 152 cm). The height is the least important measurement because most of a parrot's movements are from side to side. A cage that is 24 inches deep by 48 inches wide (61 × 122 cm) or 30 inches deep by 36 inches wide (76 × 91 cm) would be much better. There is no such thing as a cage that is too big! Eclectus parrots are enthusiastic eaters and can easily become overweight and sedentary if they don't get plenty of exercise. The best way to encourage activity is by giving them the largest cage you possibly can and filling it with toys, perches, ropes, and swings. This is especially important if family members are gone much of the day and the bird's time out of its cage is limited. A large cage is expensive, but when the cost is divided over the many years that you plan to own your bird, it will seem more reasonable (for more on cages, see chapter beginning on page 25).

Talking Ability

A parrot should not be purchased with the idea that it must become an accomplished talker. Many African Greys, the most gifted mimics of all, are content to beep like the microwave oven and whistle for the dog. They are delightful pets and loved by their owners, though they might never utter a word. Eclectus parrots are capable of becoming good talkers with a clear, human quality to their voice and will often use words appropriate to the situation. This is a highly individual trait however, and Eclectus possess many other attributes that are just as endearing. Many young birds do not begin to show an interest in talking until after their first year.

Human Allergies to Bird Dander

If anyone in the family suffers from allergies it would be wise for them to spend some time around birds before committing to parrot ownership. Eclectus do not create feather dust in the same way that cockatoos and African Greys do, but there is dander associated with feather production just as there is with animal hair. There are air cleaners and filtration systems available that are capable of removing excess dust and dander from the air. An avian veterinarian should be able to recommend types of units that have been helpful to clients.

BUYING AN ECLECTUS PARROT

The pet quality of a baby Eclectus is directly affected by the way in which it is raised. Choose a breeder or bird shop that considers the welfare of the young bird more important than making a profit.

A Baby or an Adult?

Buying a weaned, properly socialized, hand-fed baby bird from a reputable source is usually the easiest way to obtain a pet Eclectus. Adult birds sometimes come on the market though, through no fault of their own, and adopting a "used" bird that needs a home is one of the most satisfying feelings a bird owner can experience. Both options are discussed in this chapter.

Where to Buy a Baby Eclectus

Everybody loves a bargain, but a bargain-priced baby parrot from a questionable source may end up costing hundreds of dollars in veterinary bills or may have been raised in such a

A Vosmaeri Eclectus (E. roratus vosmaeri) female. Note the lack of a distinct line of separation between the red and deep lavender of the neck and belly. The yellow V-shaped undertail coverts and wide yellow tail band further differentiate this subspecies from the others.

way that its pet potential is compromised. Keep in mind that you are shopping for a lifelong companion. Take your time, do your homework, and decide exactly what you are looking for in a bird shop or breeder.

Avian veterinarians: First, locate an avian veterinarian (see page 53). You will need his or her services eventually for well-bird checkups and in the event of an illness or an emergency, and an emergency is not the time to begin hunting for an avian specialist. Avian veterinarians are familiar with the better breeders and bird shops because these breeders and shops are more likely to spend money on routine veterinary care. If your veterinarian cannot recommend anyone with Eclectus, ask for the names of other avian veterinarians you can contact.

Bird clubs: Bird clubs can be good sources of information for locating Eclectus breeders.

Bird magazines: Bird magazines and Eclectus societies and specialty sites on the Internet often have breeder listings, but keep in mind that an appealing ad is not a guarantee of quality or honesty. It is unwise to purchase a bird sight unseen.

Choosing an Eclectus Breeder

Questions to Ask

✔ Keep a notebook with questions that you intend to ask each breeder about his or her baby birds and to remind you what the answers were. Ask for references as well as the names and phone numbers of people who have purchased his or her Eclectus babies. Reputable breeders are committed to finding good homes for their baby birds and will welcome talking to someone who is interested in more than just finding the best price. Cross anyone off your list who refuses to give you this information or is reluctant to answer questions about their birds. If you feel comfortable with the person, check their references and call their customers.

✔ Ask what sort of written health guarantee comes with each baby and if any veterinarian checks or disease testing is done.

✔ Ask whether eggs are pulled for artificial incubation, or if parent birds are allowed to hatch and care for their chicks before they are removed for hand-feeding. This will give you an idea of the mind-set of the breeder. Eclectus are usually excellent parents and nobody gets tiny babies off to a good start better than Mama Eclectus. Breeders who routinely remove and artificially incubate eggs to encourage hens to lay again are more concerned with production than with the well-being of their breeding stock and young birds.

✔ Ask what method the breeder uses to feed chicks. *Gavage* or *tube feeding,* whereby the hand-feeding formula is put directly into the baby's crop via a long metal or rubber tube pushed down its throat, or *power feeding,* in which a syringe is used to quickly force a full measure of formula into the crop at one time, are fast, impersonal ways of feeding baby parrots. They are used by large commercial bird farms and by breeders who simply have too many birds and too little time. Young birds fed in this manner do not see or taste the food and may have problems later learning to eat by themselves. They are also at risk of aspiration and pneumonia as a result of food being forced into the windpipe. A baby Eclectus can be fed with either a spoon or a syringe, but the food should always be placed in its mouth. The baby should be given plenty of time to taste its food and to enjoy the feeding process.

✔ Ask if babies are completely weaned before they are sold. Run, don't walk, if anyone offers to sell you a baby Eclectus that is still dependent on hand-feedings on the premise that it will bond more strongly to the person doing the feeding. This is untrue of any baby parrot, and particularly flawed in the case of Eclectus. Eclectus babies are sensitive and show a high degree of awareness of their surroundings. They tend to become fearful, anxious, or aggressive when changes are made in their routine, environment, or hand-feeder. They are among the most difficult and time-consuming parrot babies to feed because they take food very slowly and do not respond well to a hurried approach. A stressed bird will often refuse food and can quickly become undernourished, stunted, and susceptible to disease. It is best if a baby Eclectus does not have to deal with major changes in its life until after weaning.

✔ Ask whether babies are *fledged.* Eclectus chicks that have learned what their wings are for are far more confident and less clumsy than those that have never flown. There is plenty of time for wing clipping after the baby has developed its flying skills.

✔ Ask how much time is spent socializing the babies. This is the time that people spend interacting with chicks in a way that will help them adjust to life as human companions. Babies raised in a small breeder's kitchen or living room are likely to receive more individual attention than those that grow up in a commercial nursery.

Breeder Concerns

Many breeders prefer to sell their young Eclectus directly to pet stores because raising parrots is incredibly labor-intensive and dealing with individuals takes up a great deal of time. They argue that shop employees have more time for weaning and socializing babies. Other breeders do not encourage visitors, preferring to conduct all business at the veterinarian's office after the young bird's health exam. They feel that they are risking theft or disease by allowing strangers to visit their home or aviary. These are valid concerns but many buyers feel that, given the amount of money involved, they would prefer to see the sort of conditions under which their baby Eclectus is being raised and socialized and to become acquainted with it while it is growing up.

Buyer Visits

Most small breeders will encourage a buyer to visit if they feel you are serious about buying a bird. They may quiz you about your expectations, cage size, and where the bird will be kept. You will probably be asked to wash your hands and perhaps don a gown or smock before touching any babies. Show consideration and avoid any possibility of disease transmission by not visiting other breeders, pet stores, or bird fairs before you arrive, and don't stay beyond your allotted time. It is unlikely that you will be given a tour of the aviary or permitted to see your baby's parents. Breeding parrots often feel threatened by strangers and may inadvertently damage eggs and chicks.

If you choose a bird that is not yet weaned, you will be asked to put down a deposit to hold it until it is ready to leave. You will probably be invited back a time or two so that you and your baby Eclectus can get to know each other. This is an excellent opportunity for a new owner to ask questions and learn how to handle the bird.

Choosing a Bird Shop

Bird specialty shops are usually a better choice than the typical pet store that carries everything from kittens and puppies to fish and reptiles, but much depends on the cleanliness of the facility and the knowledge and honesty of the staff. If they assure you that a sensitive species such as an African Grey is likely to enjoy being handled by small children, or that a large noisy cockatoo or macaw is a perfect apartment pet, look elsewhere.

Questions to Ask

✔ Are the birds fed a pelleted diet with fresh fruit and vegetables or are they given mostly seeds?

✔ Are the water dishes clean?

✔ Are cage papers changed daily?

✔ Are young, unweaned baby birds kept in a different area of the shop where people can't touch them without staff supervision?

✔ Are all of the birds protected from abuse by unruly children and ignorant adults?

A bird shop can be a good place to purchase an Eclectus if the store is clean and the staff is caring and knowledgeable. Baby Eclectus parrots should always be completely weaned before they are sold.

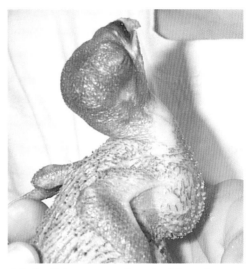

A baby Eclectus must be raised in a clean, stress-free environment if it is to become a healthy, happy adult. This chick is 16 days old.

It is normal for baby Eclectus to be temporarily nippy and suspicious of strangers. This will pass after the chick is weaned and begins to develop confidence.

Young Eclectus chicks are sensitive and aware of their surroundings. They are easily stressed by changes in their routine or environment.

This male Eclectus displays begging behavior when he sees food being prepared.

Eclectus enjoy being around children who have been taught respect for animals.

Bird Fairs

Bird fairs or marts, where breeders and vendors come together to display their birds, cages, and other supplies for sale to the public, are *not* good places to purchase a baby bird. Young birds, particularly Eclectus, are severely stressed by these events and their immature immune systems cannot protect them from the disease risk present whenever many birds share the same airspace. Babies are put further at risk when they are held or touched by admirers and prospective buyers who have recently handled other birds.

What to Look for When Buying a Baby Eclectus

The Baby Eclectus Personality

Some pet stores and bird shops prefer not to deal with Eclectus because at the same time other baby parrots are at their sweetest, cuddliest, and most saleable, young Eclectus often

CHECKLIST

Indications of Good Health in an Eclectus Parrot

1 Sleek and shiny feathers
2 Active and playful
3 Eyes bright, wide open, and alert
4 Feathers around the nares, or nostrils, clean and dry
5 Vent clean and dry with no adhering droppings

become temporarily suspicious and nippy toward strangers. This is probably fortunate because they are much less likely to end up an impulse purchase for someone with little idea of what parrot ownership entails!

Go slowly when handling a baby Eclectus. Talk gently and softly and explain what you are going to do rather than just swooping down and picking it up. The decision-making process in baby Eclectus tends to be slow and deliberate. It may contemplate your hand for a minute or two before stepping up.

Don't be put off by a baby that shows a little "attitude" toward you, a stranger, if it is obviously comfortable with the people it is most familiar with. There is evidence that once they leave the nest, baby Eclectus in the wild receive less parental nurturing than many other baby parrots. This initial wariness may be nature's way of protecting them from harm. Baby Eclectus mellow considerably after weaning. They become curious, playful, and affectionate as they gradually develop confidence in themselves and their abilities. Knowledgeable breeders and shops do not sell Eclectus babies until they have reached this stage in their lives, which can be anywhere from four to seven months old.

Feeding and Weaning Methods

A young Eclectus in the wild is completely reliant on its parents for food until it has left the nest and learned flying and foraging skills. Hand-raised birds are often encouraged to begin feeding themselves at a much younger age than nature intended. This does no harm, providing the feeder remembers that a hungry baby parrot becomes devoid of natural curiosity and the desire to explore new food choices and instead becomes intent only on getting its parents' attention. Weaning is a natural, *gradual* process and hand-feedings should never be withheld with the intent of forcing a baby parrot to eat by itself.

Baby Eclectus generally wean, or no longer require hand-feeding, at three or four months old. Weaning should not be done by the calendar, however, because every bird is different and some learn to feed themselves sooner than others. It is always best if baby parrots are permitted to wean at their own pace, and this is best accomplished by introducing them to a large variety of soft food such as dark green and yellow vegetables, fruit, cooked, dried beans, rice, and pasta, along with avian pellets and some seeds. Many modern aviculturists have discovered the benefits of using their fingers to offer warm, moist foods to weaning youngsters and this can easily be taught to new owners. All parrots enjoy occasional hand-feedings long after they are all grown up.

Was the Baby Fledged?

There is a short window of time in a young bird's life when the desire to fly overwhelms every other need, and learning to fly is easy and natural. This is known as *fledging*. Once flight skills become second nature to the bird, they are never forgotten.

For a long time it was assumed that a bird would not miss what it had never known and young domestic parrots' flight feathers were routinely clipped before they learned what their wings were for. Baby Eclectus are naturally clumsy, and with little understanding of how to use their wings for balance; many remained fearful of climbing or playing on moving swings and ropes. It was common to see young birds with many broken and damaged tail feathers

TIP

Flight

It is important to understand that wind currents may enable a bird with properly clipped wings to gain altitude outdoors. *Never take a bird outside unless it is in a cage or carrier.*

from falls, and still others that began plucking their remaining feathers from pain or frustration.

It should be remembered that flying is an integral part of a bird's sense of self and well-being, and even though most parrot owners in this country prefer not to keep their pets permanently flighted, it is important that a bird know that its wings, even when clipped, will prevent falls, increase balance, and simply make play such as running, climbing, and swinging more exhilarating.

Eclectus are naturally strong fliers and it takes only a few weeks for a youngster to master sufficient flying skills to instill lasting confidence. The baby can then undergo a progressive wing clip, whereby the flight feathers are gradually cut back over a period of several days or weeks until the desired effect is obtained. A youngster should *always* be left with enough flight feathers to enable it to glide gently to the floor from its cage top or playstand (for more on wing clipping, see page 50).

Determining the Health of a Baby Eclectus

Determining the health of a living creature can be a tricky issue for both buyer and seller. Horror stories abound concerning unsuspecting

A Grand Eclectus female
(E. roratus roratus).

The only undamaged feathers on this bird's body are the ones it can't reach. Feather plucking can be caused by stress or health factors and can be difficult to stop once the behavior becomes habit.

An Eclectus that squats low on its perch with quivering wings held away from its body is begging. It may want food, attention, or to be moved to another location.

No other species of parrot exhibits such striking sexual dimorphism, or difference between the sexes. Eclectus males are primarily green, while the females are various shades of red and deep blue or violet.

buyers who bought baby parrots that became sick or died a short time later from preexisting conditions, and purchasers who carelessly or unknowingly exposed a healthy baby to disease. Most pet shops and some breeders routinely combine baby birds from different sources, and a single diseased individual can easily infect the others. Budgies, lovebirds, and cockatiels, for instance, are notorious for carrying diseases that are a much more serious matter for larger parrots such as Eclectus, and few breeders or pet shops can afford the expense of having the smaller birds tested for disease. It is important that your new baby Eclectus be seen by an avian veterinarian either just before or immediately after the purchase.

Written health guarantees: Before visiting a breeder or bird store, ask about their written health guarantees. They should be willing to guarantee that a baby bird won't die within a specific length of time from a disease that it contracted before it was sold. If the bird dies, it is usually the responsibility of the buyer to have a necropsy, or animal autopsy, performed by a veterinarian to determine the cause of death.

Veterinary examinations: Responsible breeders and bird shops will have every bird examined by an avian veterinarian either before it comes into the store or before the buyer takes it home. The buyer should then have his or her own veterinarian follow up with whatever testing is necessary based on the disease prevalence in that area and any previous experience with the seller. Whether or not the seller has the birds checked by a veterinarian, he or she should be willing to guarantee in writing that he or she will take the bird back and refund the purchase price if it does not pass whatever tests are deemed necessary by your veterinarian. If a successful exam is part of the sales agreement, there will probably be a time limit of two or three days, so be sure to make the appointment with the veterinarian before you pick up the bird. Keep in mind that the results of some tests may take a week or more, and this should be mentioned in the agreement.

Adopting or Buying an Adult Eclectus

There can be a great deal of satisfaction derived from giving an older Eclectus a home, providing it doesn't have health or behavior problems that go beyond your experience or ability to deal with. The cost of an adult bird is usually well below the price of a baby and may or may not include a suitable cage. Parrots are often offered for sale through newspaper and Internet ads, bird club newsletters, bird fairs, and on consignment in pet shops.

Rescue and adoption organizations: Reputable parrot rescue and rehabilitation and adoption organizations are excellent places to find displaced birds. Unwanted and mistreated birds, or birds whose owners can no longer provide for them, are fostered by member volunteers until suitable homes become available. You can be confident that the well-being of the bird comes first and you will be told everything that is known about the parrot's history, health, and personality before you take it home. Some organizations will require you to attend a class on bird care and may ask to visit your home to be sure you have a suitable cage and toys and that any other birds you own are well cared for and healthy. Adoption fees are reasonable and generally reflect whatever veterinary costs have been incurred.

One of the best ways of supplying good nutrition to Eclectus parrots is to feed them sprouted seeds. For directions on sprouting, see page 42.

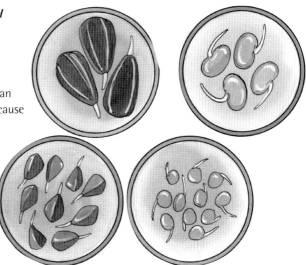

Individuals: Purchasing a parrot from an individual becomes more problematic because the seller may be reluctant to reveal the true reason that the bird is for sale. An Eclectus is often quiet and watchful when strangers are present and it can be difficult to assess its personality or identify a possible behavior problem. Most parrots are reluctant to go to people they don't know, but should readily step up on their owner's hand.

Nutrition and Health

What sort of diet is the bird accustomed to? If fed primarily seeds, it will have to be converted to a better diet as soon as possible. The most common reason for poor health and feather condition in pet parrots is inadequate nutrition.

External parasites such as mites and lice are rarely found in parrots. If the feathers on its head are perfect but those on its body are patchy, chewed, or have areas of skin showing, the bird is plucking, or overpreening its feathers. Feather abuse can be physical or behavioral in origin (stress is a common cause in Eclectus parrots), and once the behavior becomes habit, it can be difficult to stop. Whatever triggered

the problem could have ceased long ago but the bird still finds comfort in the behavior. A plucking bird is not necessarily unhappy and could still be an affectionate companion for the compassionate person who can overlook its appearance and appreciate it for the individual that it is. Eclectus have been known to stop plucking when their lives became less stressful, they began receiving the attention they need, or were put on a proper diet.

Age

Parrots are naturally long-lived and the age of a new bird need not be an important consideration if it has been well cared for.

CAGES AND EQUIPMENT

A cage should be a parrot's castle. Its size, shape, location and furnishings will help determine if your Eclectus feels safe and happy. A portable playstand will enable the bird to accompany you in other areas of the house.

Cage Location

Parrots are flock animals that derive comfort and safety from being near other creatures. It will be better to find a way to allow your Eclectus to share your living space than to relegate it to an out-of-the-way room. An Eclectus also needs to feel safe and secure.

✔ The cage should be placed against a wall or in a corner so that the bird has a place to retreat if it feels threatened. This will also prevent people from walking all around the cage—something most birds find disconcerting.

✔ The climate of your home is not of great importance. Your Eclectus will soon become accustomed to whatever temperatures you find comfortable. We know now that parrots aren't any more sensitive to drafts than we are, but obvious temperature extremes—places close to heating and air conditioning vents or hot, sunny windows—should be avoided.

Vosmaeri Eclectus (E. roratus vosmaeri) male and female from the northern and central Moluccan Islands.

✔ Don't put the cage where people can come up on the bird suddenly and startle it without meaning to, or next to the front door where it will be forced into close encounters with strangers.

✔ A window can be a source of enjoyment and entertainment for parrots providing they are far enough from it not to feel threatened by what is going on outside.

✔ Don't place the cage next to the television set. Parrots need about ten hours of sleep each night or they can be grumpy and irritable just like people.

✔ Covering the cage at night is a good idea if family members are on different schedules and the bird may not get enough sleep.

✔ A smaller sleeping cage in a quiet room is a good solution if the main cage is in an area that is bright and noisy much of the time.

Proper Lighting

Although Eclectus are native to warm, sunny, tropical climates, they adapt easily to the lower temperatures of our homes. Good lighting is important, however, and window glass blocks most of the health-giving ultraviolet rays of the sun. A *full-spectrum* light designed for plants and animals is the next best thing to natural sunlight and should be positioned directly over the cage. Follow the manufacturer's recommendations for distance.

Choosing a Cage

The cage and its furnishings are important to your Eclectus' security, safety, comfort, health, and happiness. A roomy cage of its own, with lots of toys and room to swing, flap its wings, and play will go a long way toward preventing serious behavior problems such as feather plucking or screaming from stress or boredom. Although many pet parrots get along well together while they are out of their cages, it is important for each bird to have its own cage.

Cage size: As discussed previously, the *minimum*-sized cage recommended for an Eclectus is 24 inches deep, 36 inches wide, and 60 inches high (61 × 91 × 152 cm). *There is no such thing as a cage that is too big!* Parrots in the wild are able to flee scary or threatening situations.

TIP

Cage Weight

Eclectus are not particularly destructive and are not likely to destroy the finish or break welds, so an extremely heavy cage isn't necessary. A bar spacing of one inch (2.5 cm) or less will prevent an Eclectus from getting its head caught.

Forcing them to confront their fears and dislikes close up, even if the object of concern is only a boisterous child or Aunt Martha's weird hat, can be a major cause of stress. A large cage provides a bit of extra room to retreat and watch the world from a safe vantage point. An Eclectus is likely to become overweight and sedentary if it considers its cage primarily a place to eat and sleep because there is little room or motivation to do anything else.

Cage styles: Cages usually come in two styles: dome tops and play tops. A dome top is preferable because it gives added height to the cage interior and an added sense of security for the occupant. It can sometimes be difficult for an owner to remove an unwilling parrot from a tall cage top, and some young Eclectus, particularly those nearing sexual maturity, may become somewhat aggressive and territorial when allowed to play on top of their cages. Parrot behavior specialists often equate altitude with attitude. That is, they feel that allowing a parrot to perch above an owner's eye level may encourage an already dominant bird to challenge authority. A separate play area, especially if it is in another room, is a much better alternative to a cage play top because it provides a new source of visual stimulation and removes any need for the bird to defend its territory.

Some manufacturers have shortened their cages to keep the play top within easy reach. This may be convenient for the owner, but it leaves the highest perch inside the cage far too low to provide a feeling of security for the occupant. A timid or sensitive bird will immediately adopt a more relaxed attitude when it is moved to a higher, less vulnerable position. An Eclectus is not likely to be happy in a cage

Cages generally come in both dome top and play top styles. The dome top is preferable because there is more useable space inside the cage and because some parrots become territorial when allowed to play on top of their cages.

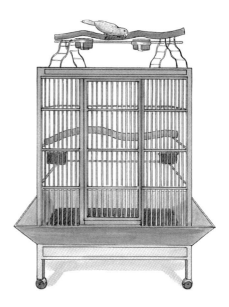

where it must sit at eye level with large dogs and small children.

Selection of Perches

Perches are as important to parrots as shoes are to people. Eclectus have small feet for their body size and they don't grip tightly with their toes, so smooth, slippery perches should be avoided. It is good to have perches of several different diameters and materials so that the parrot's feet get lots of exercise and the bird can choose comfortable places to sit. Most

birds use the highest perch in the cage for sleeping, so it is important that it be comfortable and secure.

Manzanita: Manzanita is an extremely smooth hardwood that even cockatoos and macaws find difficult to destroy. It is too slippery for Eclectus to grip easily unless the diameter is small enough for the bird to wrap its toes most of the way around. Larger manzanita perches will have to be roughened before they are put in the cage. This can be accomplished with a wood rasp or an inexpensive rotary rasp attachment for an electric drill.

Dowels: Wooden dowels, ¾ inch to 1¾ inch (19–44 mm), work well and can be roughened if necessary. Like manzanita, they are easily cleaned.

Rope: Rope perches made of thick, flexible braided cotton can be attached in corners and from cage tops where straight perches won't

Cement perches come in many shapes and sizes, and reduce the need for toenail trimming by keeping sharp nail tips worn down.

fit. They are washable, comfortable, provide secure footing, and make good sleeping perches. Rope is also a good choice for the swings that Eclectus love so much. Frayed or worn rope perches and toys should be kept trimmed so they don't entangle legs and toes.

Cholla cactus wood: Cholla cactus wood from the American Southwest has an open, spongelike surface that makes even large diameters easy to grip. Its porosity makes it somewhat difficult to clean, so cholla perches are best positioned high in the cage and away

Cholla cactus perches are a favorite of Eclectus because they are comfortable and easy to grip.

Perches made of soft wood encourage healthy chewing exercise.

Eclectus parrots should be encouraged to exercise. This bird enjoys flapping his wings while his owner holds his feet.

Manzanita perches are popular for parrots, but their hard, slippery surface can be difficult for an Eclectus to grip.

A cement perch swing, acrylic toys that shake and rattle, and a homemade chew toy of soft wood and leather encourage Eclectus parrots to play.

from food dishes to avoid soiling. It is an ideal sleeping perch for Eclectus.

Cement: Grooming perches and swings made of textured cement are designed to keep the sharp tips of parrot's toenails worn down. They reduce the need for frequent nail trimming and Eclectus seem to like cleaning their beaks on the rough surface. To be effective, cement perches need to be positioned near food and water dishes or other frequented spots. They are easily removed for cleaning.

Plastic: Tough PVC plastic perches are sometimes used for large destructive parrots, but they can be slippery and there is little reason to recommend them for Eclectus when natural materials are better and readily available. Metal pipe or conduit is not a suitable perch material.

The above ready-made perches are available from bird stores and bird supply catalogs, but the best perches are probably the ones you make yourself from natural green tree branches. Pick limbs with textured bark and varied shapes that will provide the bird with good footing and hours of happy peeling and chewing. Avoid trees from orchards and roadsides where pesticides are routinely used. Plant toxicity is rare in parrots, but if you are unsure of the type of wood, remove any leaves, buds, or blossoms before putting it in the cage.

Outfitting the Cage

Perches

When setting up the cage, it is not necessary that the main perch lead directly to food and water bowls. It is good exercise for the Eclectus to climb across the cage bars to a short perch near each dish and this may prevent it from dunking everything it eats in its water. The cage should have lots of perches to encourage climbing and at least one wood or rope swing.

Dishes

There should be at least three dishes in the cage—one for dry food and pellets, one for soft foods such as fruit and vegetables, and one for water. Try to have an extra set of dishes so that one can be used while the other is being washed. Food and water dishes should be washed daily with hot soap and water.

Toys

It is critical not to overlook the importance of toys to an intelligent, active creature that is confined to one place for long periods of time. Toys need not be expensive and the best ones are often those made by the parrot's owner. They should be as varied as possible, using such materials as soft wood, rope, leather, paper, and small soft wooden beads and blocks that will encourage chewing. Eclectus are not as destructive as other similarly sized parrots but they love to shake their toys and bat them about. A few colorful acrylic toys with lots of small, noisy, moveable parts are also good. Take care to choose toys with your bird's

Many types of portable playstands are available that allow an Eclectus to accompany its owner in different areas of the home. They should be equipped with food, water dishes, and toys.

safety in mind. Avoid those that have open loops, key rings, and snap hooks that could trap heads, toes, beaks, or leg bands. Be sure to trim cotton and sisal rope as it unravels so it can't entangle toes.

A good way to keep a parrot interested in its toys is to have plenty of extras and rotate them every few days. Your Eclectus will be delighted when given a toy that it hasn't seen for a couple of weeks.

Swings

Eclectus love bouncy, round, or spiral-shaped swings made of heavy braided rope over flexible wire cores. They provide sure footing and the movement encourages active play. Slender green twigs from safe trees and shrubs can be hung in the cage or woven between the bars. Eclectus will spend hours happily peeling the tender bark.

Some parrots are fearful or suspicious of brand-new objects that suddenly appear in their cage. Introduce new toys and perches slowly by placing them on the floor a few feet from the cage and allowing the bird time to get use to them.

Playstands and Gyms

Many parrot owners have playstands or play gyms in other rooms or a portable one that is easily moved so their birds can accompany them around the house. This opportunity to follow its flock will be welcomed by an Eclectus and will greatly add to your enjoyment of your bird. Pet parrots are also likely to be less territorial and more easily handled when away from their cage. Like the cage, the playstand should have comfortable, easy-to-grip perches and interesting toys, as well as dishes for food and water.

Travel Carriers

With birds increasing in popularity as pets, many new styles of containers for safely transporting parrots have come on the market. Few provide the protection and security needed by Eclectus better than the familiar and readily available plastic cat and dog carriers with metal doors and latch mechanisms available at any pet supply outlet. Clear acrylic and open wire mesh carriers are suitable for birds that have become accustomed to frequent excursions, but most Eclectus prefer to watch the world go by from a safe, enclosed place. If you choose one of the open types, be sure to get a cloth cover for it. If the bird is likely to be spending more than two or three hours at a time in its carrier, such as during long car trips or nights in hotel rooms, it would be good to get a size larger and fasten a wooden perch an inch or so from the bottom. If you plan to travel with your parrot in the cabin of a commercial airliner you will need a special carrier that will fit under the seats, but it will be much too small and cramped for any other use. (Make certain that birds are permitted in the passenger cabin before arriving at the airport!)

There should be a carrier available for each bird in the house in the event of fire, tornado, hurricane, or other emergency, as well as for routine trips to the veterinarian. Two parrots should never be put in the same carrier. Stress or fear can cause aggression and injuries, even between friends.

An ordinary plastic pet carrier is easy to keep warm with a heating pad and makes a good hospital cage for sick or injured birds until veterinary help can be obtained.

FEEDING ECLECTUS PARROTS

It is often said that Eclectus live to eat. It is especially important that they are given foods that will enable them to live long, healthy lives. Fresh fruit and vegetables should be fed on a daily basis.

Enthusiastic Eaters

There is little doubt that the path to every Eclectus parrot's heart is by way of its stomach. The author's pair of Solomon Island Eclectus, Poppy and Sage, observe food preparations in her kitchen with flashing eyes and excited wing flapping. When they emerge blissfully from their food bowl, their faces covered with warm rice or sweet potatoes, it is hard to imagine where Eclectus got the reputation for being stodgy and aloof.

According to Joseph Forshaw, the food of wild Eclectus includes fruits, nuts, seeds, berries, leaf buds, new leaf shoots, blossoms, and nectar, all of which are procured in the treetops. While it is rarely possible to duplicate the diet of parrots in the wild, Eclectus enjoy such a wide variety of foods that it is usually easy to get them to eat a healthy diet. They are such enthusiastic eaters, in fact, that it is especially important to choose their foods carefully so they don't become too fat.

There are few things more important to an Eclectus parrot than food!

It should be kept in mind that when parrots develop poor eating habits it is invariably the fault of the owner. We love our Eclectus and want it to be happy, so we tend to make its favorite foods the bulk of its diet. If we also give the bird more kinds of food each day than it can possibly eat, there is little reason for it to try anything new.

Types of Food

Pellets or Seeds?

For as long as people have been keeping birds in captivity, our pet parrots' most common health problems have been and still are directly related to poor nutrition. It had always been assumed that because canaries, finches, and budgerigars thrived on seeds, it must be the proper thing to feed all parrots. While a variety of seeds in small amounts are a welcome treat for most psittacines, we now know that an all-seed diet is deficient in almost every nutrient except fat. Poor nutrition is rarely listed as the cause of death of pet parrots because most of them succumb to secondary infections common to birds with weakened resistance and the inability of the body to heal itself through normal cellular regeneration.

Many parrot owners are lulled into thinking they are doing the right thing by purchasing attractive vitamin-fortified seed mixes containing colorful pellets and dried fruit and nuts. Often these products are advertised as supplying complete nutrition for parrots. Unfortunately, the vitamins are usually added to the seed hulls that the bird removes before it consumes the kernel inside. The parrot then tosses the pellets on the floor while it hunts through the bowl for its favorite high-fat nuts and oil seeds.

Dried fruits are largely sugar and contain too few nutrients to remedy the situation, and the addition of fresh fruits and table foods a few times a week cannot balance a primarily seed diet. You can put all sorts of healthy food in your bird's dishes but they won't do a bit of good if it doesn't eat them. And that is what usually happens when parrots have access to all the seed they want.

With all of the excellent pelleted hookbill diets on the market today, there is no longer any reason to feed parrots large amounts of seed. Most pellet manufacturers take care to formulate their products according to the most up-to-date research on psittacine nutrition. For the first time in the history of bird keeping it is easy for busy owners to provide a balanced diet for their pet and breeder birds. While pellets are not perfect and should not be fed exclusively, they help us provide the essential nutrients that our birds need.

Many Eclectus owners report that their birds seem unusually sensitive to chemical additives in their foods, so it's best to avoid pellets containing artificial food colors and dyes. Ask your avian veterinarian to recommend a suitable brand.

Mixes and Mashes

Before avian pellets became popular, cooked mixes and mashes were the best way for aviculturists to supply good nutrition to their parrots. Eclectus enjoy them so much that many breeders and pet owners continue to cook for their birds.

Vegetables and Fruits

Eclectus parrots are thought to be particularly sensitive to inadequate levels of vitamin A and fiber in their diet.

Vegetables: Deeply pigmented vegetables are high in beta carotene, which is converted by the bird's body to vitamin A. Because their bodies don't utilize this natural form of vitamin A

Cooked Bean, Rice, and Corn Mix

Mix together:
✔ Two 20-ounce (560-g) bags of frozen corn
✔ One 20-ounce (560-g) bag of frozen peas and carrots
✔ Five cups of dried beans (any kind or a mixture), cooked, drained well and cooled. (Beans are more attractive to Eclectus if they are crisp/tender, not mushy.)
✔ Five cups of cooked brown rice, cooled.
✔ Two cups of cooked vegetable rotini pasta, drained well and cooled.

Put one-half cup portions of the above mixture into individual plastic bags and freeze. Remove one package per bird each evening and thaw in the refrigerator. Warm before feeding.

Holders that allow fruit and vegetables to be suspended in the cage are a good way to coax Eclectus parrots to try new foods.

unless there is a metabolic need for it, there is no danger of overfeeding, as might be the case with vitamin supplements. In general, the more deeply colored the vegetable, the richer the source of total nutrients. Some vegetables have moderate protein levels and are good vitamin and mineral sources as well. They are generally high in fiber, low in fat, and are precisely what our domestic Eclectus parrots need to preserve their health, longevity, and incredible depth of color. Conversely, very light and pale vegetables such as iceberg lettuce and celery are rather poor sources of nutrients, being comprised mainly of water and fiber.

Fruits: Most fruits consist largely of water, sugar, and fiber, but Eclectus seem unusually well adapted for extracting their limited nutrients. Some seasonal fruits that Eclectus enjoy are cantaloupe, apricots, cranberries, blueberries, sweet and sour cherries, pomegranates, and especially papaya, which, according to Lynn Devan and other early breeders of Eclectus, is one of the keys to keeping them healthy, happy, and in good breeding condition. Fruit with dark yellow flesh is more likely to contain significant amounts of beta carotene, a vitamin A precursor.

Other Healthy Foods

Other healthy foods that your Eclectus parrot will enjoy are cooked brown or white rice, cooked dried peas, beans, and lentils, cooked beets, baked potatoes, defrosted green peas, cantaloupe seeds, dried unsalted pumpkin seeds, dried unsweetened cereals, and all kinds of cooked or dried uncooked pasta, as well as the following:
✔ Sprouted seeds of all kinds are high in nutrients and excellent food for parrots.

TIP

Preparing Fruit and Vegetables

Be sure to thoroughly wash all fresh fruit and vegetables to remove traces of pesticides, and chop them on a cutting board that is not used for meat and poultry. You might consider purchasing organic produce if you live in an area where it is readily available.

Poor-quality sprouts can harbor harmful molds and bacteria, however, so if you decide to grow your own, start with fresh organic seeds and beans intended for sprouting and available at most health food stores. Sprouted seeds are at their most nutritious stage and are best fed to parrots when the sprout first emerges and is less than ¼ inch (6 mm) long.

✔ Corn is a hands-down favorite of most Eclectus parrots. Defrosted sweet corn is appreciated as is fresh corn on the cob cut into wheels, or dried, whole shelled field corn, or popcorn soaked overnight and boiled or microwaved until slightly softened.

✔ Well-cooked slivers of lean chicken, turkey, and fish are relished, as are cooked chicken rib bones and marrowbones with cartilage and bits of meat attached. There is no need to worry that a parrot might swallow bone splinters.

Food preparation is the high point of the day for an Eclectus parrot!

✔ Eclectus especially enjoy scrambled eggs and chopped hard-boiled eggs, shells included.

✔ Spray millet is a good low-fat treat that will keep your bird happily occupied for hours and satisfy its desire for seeds.

✔ Eclectus parrots will eat nuts that have been cracked or removed from their shells; however, it is probably best not to feed too many. Since most Eclectus have difficulty opening even an almond shell, it is clear that mature nuts were never meant to be a large part of their diet. Like other parrots that were designed for a high-energy lifestyle in the wild, Eclectus are attracted to nuts, oil seeds, and other high-fat foods even though such fare is too rich for their role as sedentary companion birds. An exception to this rule is the young bird under two years old that is still growing and can utilize some extra fat in its diet. Dried fruit and nut mixes with their extremely high fat and sugar content are the equivalent of bird candy and should not be fed on a daily basis.

Food Holders

Bird stores and supply outlets sell stainless steel skewers that hold fresh rounds of corn on the cob, apple slices, or whole jalapeno peppers, shish kabob style. Smaller foods such as cherries, fresh broccoli florets, and pieces of spray millet can be contained in round plastic carousel treat holders that are also suspended from the cage top. Eclectus love to play with their food and this is a good way to encourage activity.

Unlike many parrots, Eclectus don't usually use their feet to hold food. They prefer to sit on or near the edge of their dish and eat with their head in the bowl so as not to drop a single crumb. Food crocks should be as large as possible, which will also help prevent food slinging by a bird that wants to see what is at the bottom of its bowl.

Note: Pellets should be fed in small amounts that a bird will eat in a day or two. Bacteria levels can build up when stale, partially eaten pellets and seeds are continually topped up. Moist, cooked foods spoil quickly, especially in warm weather, and should be removed after two or three hours.

Introducing New Foods

While some parrot species tend to be somewhat finicky and reluctant to try new foods, this is rarely the case with Eclectus. Still, it is

CHECKLIST

Vegetables Naturally High in Beta-carotene

One or more of the following vegetables should be fed to all Eclectus parrots on a daily basis.

1 Carrots (cooked and raw, grated, diced, or whole)
2 Sweet potatoes, yams, winter squash, and pumpkin (baked or microwaved in their skins)
3 Red, yellow, and green bell and hot peppers with seeds, Swiss chard, dandelion greens, carrot tops, collard greens, mustard greens, and kale (raw)
4 Broccoli leaves and buds (slightly steamed or raw)

Vegetables and fruit naturally high in beta-carotene should be fed to Eclectus parrots on a daily basis.

part of the survival strategy of all parrots to be suspicious of anything new and different. If your Eclectus growls angrily and throws the expensive blueberries you just bought out of his bowl, it doesn't mean that he doesn't like blueberries. He simply isn't about to bite into something he has never seen before. Don't overwhelm him with a bowlful of the new food. Begin by tucking small bits of it into food that he likes. Continue to offer small amounts *every day* until he becomes accustomed to seeing it and decides that he likes it. It will help if he sees his owner or other birds munching enthusiastically on the new food. Parrots don't have particularly well-developed taste buds and their apparent dislike for something new is usually because it is different in texture and appearance from foods they are familiar with.

Converting an older bird from seed to pellets is accomplished in the same way:

✔ Each day mix two level tablespoons of mixed seeds and one level tablespoon of pellets in the same bowl. Keep the amounts small so that you can easily determine what gets eaten, and keep the cage papers changed so that you know what ends up on the bottom.

✔ Mix a few pellets into his bowl of fruit and veggies or soft food or soak them in fruit juice. You can even hide pellets in his toys.

✔ After a week or two begin removing the oil seeds (sunflower and safflower) from the seed mix, leaving the cereal grains such as millet, canary seed, oat groats, and buckwheat in his dish.

✔ Gradually decrease the seeds and increase the pellets until he is eating the pellets, being careful not to put more food in his bowl than he can clean up in one day. Be sure to feed plenty of fresh vegetables and fruit during this time.

✔ Once the bird is eating pellets, you can continue to offer the low-fat cereal grains two or three times a week.

Signs of Dietary Deficiencies and Obesity

Poor feather condition is often the first clue that something is wrong with an Eclectus parrot's diet. A bird with dull, greasy-looking feathers streaked in black or a sprinkling of orange and yellow feathers is probably suffering from a dietary deficiency. Some medications have also been known to cause temporary changes in feather color. As an Eclectus molts and new feathers replace old ones, it should soon become apparent if changes in nutrition have been for the better. A bird that doesn't respond to an improved diet should be seen by an avian veterinarian.

Many people don't realize that their pet is overweight because, unlike other parrots, Eclectus build up dangerous fat pads within their abdominal cavities instead of just beneath the skin where it would be easily recognized. When you bathe your Eclectus, thoroughly wet and separate the feathers covering the center lower abdomen so that you can see the skin. A layer of subcutaneous fat will make the skin appear yellow and is an indication that the bird is also carrying too much internal fat. Obesity is most often a problem in female Eclectus.

Foods to Avoid

Most healthy "people foods" are relished by parrots and are safe for your Eclectus. There are a few exceptions listed below.

✔ Chocolate. This contains the active ingredients theophylline and caffeine, which even in small amounts can cause hyperactivity, vomiting, diarrhea, heart problems, seizures, and death.

✔ Avocados. Some varieties are definitely toxic to birds. It is still uncertain what part of the avocado causes the problem, so to be safe this fruit should be avoided.

✔ Caffeine. Food and drinks containing caffeine are dangerous for birds.

✔ Alcohol. No beer, mixed drinks, or any products containing alcohol should be given to birds.

✔ Peanuts. These grow in the ground and very often contain invisible fungi-produced toxins that can be harmful to birds. Since it is impossible to tell which peanuts are affected just by looking, it is best to avoid them entirely. "Tree" nuts such as almonds are a better choice. Never give dusty or moldy food of any kind to your Eclectus.

✔ Apple seeds and fruit pits. Parrots love these, and while there aren't enough seeds in a single piece of fruit to harm a bird the size of an Eclectus, theoretically they contain enough cyanide to be harmful if eaten in quantity. Interestingly, the author has not been able to find a single reported incident of fruit seed toxicity in parrots.

✔ Lactose (milk sugar). Milk and milk products are not toxic, but those that contain significant amounts of lactose may cause diarrhea if fed in large amounts. Cheese, yogurt, and other cultured milk products contain little or no lactose and are safe for birds. Cheese is okay as a treat, but most kinds contain too much fat and salt to be fed very often.

✔ Sugar, salt, and fat. Foods such as potato chips, candy, and butter should be fed in *very* limited amounts or not at all.

✔ Artificial food colors and dyes. Brightly colored pellets and treats are a marketing ploy to attract people. There have been reports of Eclectus parrots with odd orange and yellow feathers that molted and grew back normally when dye-saturated pellets were removed from their diet.

Grit

Seed-eating birds of all kinds eat tiny stones and pebbles that lodge in the muscular ventriculus, or gizzard, where they aid in crushing seeds and grains during the digestion process. Sometimes out of boredom or ill health, Eclectus will overeat grit, causing a very dangerous condition whereby the ventriculus becomes impacted with stones. The experts are currently divided about whether parrots on primarily pelleted diets need grit at all. Since wild Eclectus parrots are rarely observed feeding near the ground and would have access to mostly soft, unripe seeds and nuts, it seems unlikely that they would require grit.

Vitamin Supplements

It is possible to give your Eclectus too much of a good thing. Recent findings suggest that relying heavily on synthetic vitamins in the form of vitamin supplements or vitamin enriched or fortified manufactured diets, pellets, seeds, treats, or table foods may cause involuntary Toe Tapping in Eclectus parrots (see Recognizing Illness, page 55). It is important that most of the nutrients in an Eclectus' diet come from fresh, natural, unprocessed foods.

Eclectus do not usually use their feet to hold and manipulate food as this cockatoo is doing. Food bowls should be large enough so the bird can eat comfortably with its head over the dish.

Water

Eclectus parrots should have clean drinking water at all times. This can be a challenge for their owners because of their habit of dipping everything they eat in their water crock. One solution is to move food and water bowls as far apart as possible. Another is to position the water dish away from the main perches to make it more difficult to carry food to it. Be especially careful to position the water bowl where it can't be fouled by the bird's droppings. Even with these precautions, water in open containers will probably need changing twice a day. Water bowls should be cleaned and scrubbed daily with hot, soapy water.

Some parrot owners favor water bottles, but bottles have disadvantages of their own. Modern water treatment facilities ensure that the bacteria level in drinking water is low enough to be safe when it comes from the tap. Tap water that sits for 24 hours at room temperature may look clean, but is most likely supporting a thriving colony of bacteria. The water in bottles must be changed daily and the bottles, including stems and stoppers, scrubbed with hot, soapy water and disinfected with a chlorine bleach solution twice a week.

If you choose to use a bottle, be certain that your bird has learned to use it before you remove its water crock. Check bottles

A female Red-sided Eclectus.

Suspending food in various kinds of holders is an excellent way to encourage active play in an Eclectus parrot.

frequently to be sure that they have not become clogged with bits of food that might restrict the flow of water. It is good to have extra water bowls or bottles so that one set can be used while the other is being washed.

Soft green branches with the bark left on make ideal perches. They encourage chewing, and the natural variations in size and shape are appealing to parrots.

Sprouting Seeds

Germination: When a dry, dormant seed is soaked in water for a few hours, natural chemical changes take place as the process of germination begins. Enzymes are released to convert stored nutrients into those needed by the new plant. The fat and starch content drops as vitamin and protein levels soar. When the tiny white root tip emerges, usually in as little as 24 to 36 hours, the living, nutrient-packed seed is ready to be fed to our birds. All that is necessary during the germination period is to keep the seeds damp and squeaky-clean by rinsing them often under fresh running water.

Seeds for sprouting: Start with organically grown, chemical-free seeds, grains, or legumes available from your health food store. Some that are easy and quick to sprout are sunflower, buckwheat, mung beans, adzuki beans, lentils, and wheat berries.

Items needed for sprouting:

✔ a medium or large fine-mesh stainless steel kitchen strainer with handle
✔ a bowl for the strainer to rest on
✔ a lid that will lie loosely over both

Method

1. Start with about ½ cup of seeds (less if your strainer is small).

2. Remove any broken or damaged seeds that could cause the rest to spoil.

3. Put the seeds in the bowl, fill it with clean tap water, and swirl them around with your hand, then pour them into the strainer. Repeat several times until the water runs clear.

4. Pour the seeds back into the bowl, cover with several inches of water, and let soak for three or four hours.

5. Drain them back into the strainer and rinse well under running tap water.

The basic steps for sprouting seeds are: 1) Wash thoroughly under running water. 2) Cover with water and soak for three or four hours. 3) Rinse well several times a day, drain, and cover loosely with a lid until the white "tails" begin to show. Seeds should be fed to your Eclectus when the sprout is less than 1/4 inch long.

6. Place the strainer so that it hangs over the bowl, resting on the rim. It should not touch the bottom of the bowl. Cover loosely with the lid.

7. Rinse at least three or four times a day—more often during warm weather—by holding the strainer under fresh running tap water. Rinsing may be done more efficiently by placing the seeds back in the bowl and running water into it, swirling the seeds around, and then pouring them back in the strainer. This should be done several times. Frequent, thorough rinsing is the key to successful sprouting.

When tiny tails begin to appear, the sprouts are ready. Drain the sprouts well or spread them out on paper towels until most of the moisture has been absorbed before feeding to your Eclectus. If sprouts are fed dry, they will stay fresh much longer in your bird's dish. Well-drained sprouts will keep in the refrigerator for several days.

Healthy sprouts have a warm, earthy smell. If they develop a sour odor, throw them out. Health food stores carry natural citrus-based products such as Grapefruit Seed Extract that can be added to the initial soak water to inhibit bacterial or fungal growth.

A Treat Jar

Commercial treat mixes made up of dried fruit and nuts contain too much sugar and fat for Eclectus. You can make your own colorful crunchy treat mix with a mixture of natural

A homemade treat jar is a healthy alternative to high-fat commercial products.

ingredients readily available at the grocer or health food store. The quantities and ingredients can vary, which is what makes them fun.

Start with a large decorative glass jar with a tightly fitting lid. Fill it with equal parts of crunchy, unsweetened breakfast cereal such as Cheerios or Rice Chex; dried banana chips; uncooked, dried vegetable pasta; small, dried, hot red peppers; popcorn—popped without butter or salt; almonds—either whole in the shell or chopped or slivered; and millet seed or a budgie or cockatiel seed mix. You may discover other dry, unsweetened, unsalted foods that will appeal to your Eclectus. Soft, dried fruits such as raisins are unsuitable for the treat jar because their moisture content is too high.

Understanding wing clipping, nail trimming, and how feathers grow is part of the fun and responsibility of owning an Eclectus parrot. It isn't difficult to learn to do this yourself.

Wings: To Clip or Not?

Wing clipping, or trimming, is not a universal practice. In Europe, pet birds are rarely clipped, yet incidents of lost parrots are unusual. The reasons for wing clipping that are so often trotted out—that flighted birds are more likely to drown in toilets, get burned on stovetops, or hit by ceiling fans—are simply not true. *Proficient* flyers are not prone to accidents. The author has watched a flighted parrot swoop down over a bowl of potato chips, hover briefly in midair while choosing one, then fly to a safe place to enjoy its prize. This is not a bird that is likely to fall into a pot of hot water!

Skilled flight, however, takes constant practice, and few pet parrots acquire the degree of competence needed to keep them out of harm's way. Most young parrots' wings are clipped before or shortly after they fledge or take their first flight, and they are never given

This male Eclectus enjoys being sprinkled with warm water at the kitchen sink. Regular baths are essential to good feather condition.

the opportunity to perfect their flying skills. *There are few things more dangerous for a bird than having the ability of flight without having first learned to control it.* The scenario is similar to that of a child who gets on a bicycle for the first time and heads down a busy street. Parrots that don't know how to control their flight, that are startled and suddenly find themselves airborne because their once clipped flight feathers have grown back, are likely to have serious accidents in the house or become lost outdoors. If they are accidentally carried outside on their owner's shoulder and end up high in a tree, they not only have fear to contend with, but are seriously handicapped by lack of flight skills. Wide-open spaces are unnerving to a bird that has never been outdoors and it is likely to flap off in a panic, eventually becoming exhausted and hopelessly lost.

A good way to accustom a parrot to being outdoors is to have it outside with you in a portable cage while you work or play. Or better yet, have a sturdy, permanent outdoor cage or aviary where the bird can safely play and enjoy the sun.

Encouraging Flight

An Eclectus with unclipped wings should be encouraged to fly as much as possible because without the agility that comes with practice, the chance of injuries are much greater. There should be several approved perches or play areas so the bird is less likely to get into trouble or cause damage. A favorite perching place of flighted parrots is the tops of open doors. These should be covered with small rugs or blankets when the bird is out of its cage, both to protect doors from chewing and to remind family members not to accidentally close them on the bird's feet. Flighted parrots should be introduced carefully to large mirrors, windows, and household pets. Also, a home with young children running in and out is not a safe place for an unclipped Eclectus.

Supervision

Having a fully flighted parrot in the house is a responsibility that the whole family must take seriously. It isn't enough just to allow your bird's flight feathers to grow out. If you are not prepared to actively encourage flight and to be continually vigilant about making your home safe for a bird that can go anywhere it pleases, your Eclectus will be better off with its wings clipped.

Because flighted parrots require constant supervision, they often end up spending more time in their cages than those that are clipped. Pet birds need and want to be with their people, but owners who might otherwise enjoy traveling or vacationing with their Eclectus are likely to leave a flighted bird at home. The author feels that, if asked to choose between the ability to fly and the opportunity to spend more time in the company of their owners, most pet Eclectus would elect to be with the people they love.

Bathing Your Eclectus

Eclectus parrots are native to humid forested areas with abundant rainfall. Dry indoor air is hard on both their skin and feathers and it is important that the moisture be replaced by regular bathing. Most Eclectus love bathing and those that don't will usually change their mind in time if baths are offered often in a nonthreatening manner.

If a bird dislikes or is unaccustomed to baths, don't soak it to the skin in the beginning. Find a spray bottle with a nozzle that will adjust to a fine mist and direct the warm spray above its head from 2 or 3 feet (61–91 cm) away so that the water rains gently down. Often the noise of a vacuum cleaner will stimulate Eclectus to bathe—perhaps reminding them of heavy rain pounding in the forest. Some pet birds prefer bathing in a shallow pan of warm water on a kitchen counter. Watching another bird splashing enthusiastically will often convince a reluctant bather that water is fun. Perches are available that fasten to the shower wall with suction cups so that a parrot can shower with its owner. Be sure that the perch isn't slippery and is positioned so the bird can move freely in and out of the spray. Quick, warm spray baths can be given daily regardless of the weather, but be sure that your Eclectus gets drenched to the skin at least once a week.

Some birds enjoy being gently wrapped in a towel after their baths, while others love the feel of a blow dryer set on low. Neither is necessary however, because your Eclectus will dry itself quickly as nature intended by shaking and preening the water from its feathers. Soaked-to-the-skin baths are best done early enough in the day so that the bird is dry by bedtime.

Note: Never use anything but pure water for bathing your Eclectus.

Understanding the Molt

Molting is the process whereby the growth of a new feather causes the shedding of an old feather. Molting tends to happen in one-year cycles, but not all of the types of feathers on a bird's body are affected in each cycle. At any one time, a bird may have feathers derived from more than one molt. Most parrots have *progressive molts*. That is, two corresponding primary feathers—one on each wing—fall out and new ones grow in their place before any more feathers are lost. A progressive molt insures that a bird will never be unable to fly as a result of being unbalanced or losing all of its feathers at once. When all of the flight feathers have been replaced, the molt will begin on another section of the bird's body, such as the head and neck. Exactly what controls the molt is not completely understood, but parrots that are housed indoors under artificial lights, or allowed to breed year-round, or those that are stressed or fed inadequate diets, may be "confused" and complete two head and neck molts in one year and a body molt the second year. It is common for parrots in an artificial environment to be wearing brand-new feathers and shabby old feathers at the same time.

Some Eclectus seem to have easy molts that are light, gradual, and hardly noticeable, while others lose clumps of head, neck, or body feathers, leaving large patches of gray down.

Many parrots seem irritable when they are growing lots of prickly, itchy new pinfeathers. Daily bathing or misting and a good diet will go a long way to relieve the stress of molting.

Restraining Your Eclectus

Wing and nail trims don't have to be stressful for a parrot if it becomes accustomed to having its wings gently spread and its flight feathers and toes touched and admired while it is being held and played with. A new flight feather can be trimmed or a sharp nail can be touched up quickly with an emery board, scarcely giving the bird time to object. If your Eclectus will not tolerate this sort of handling it will be necessary to restrain it in a towel.

✔ Gently wrap the bird in a large bath towel making sure that its face is covered. Birds are highly visual creatures and they are also prey animals. Being held in this extremely vulnerable position by an owner who is wearing an unfamiliar look of intense concentration in his or her eyes can be a frightening experience.

✔ Locate the back of the bird's head through the towel and circle the bird's neck directly under the lower *mandible,* or beak, with your thumb and index finger. This will keep the parrot from "swapping ends" under the towel, and prevent you from being bitten. *Be careful not to apply pressure to the bird's chest. It does not have a diaphragm as mammals do and needs to raise and lower its sternum to breathe.*

Many pet parrots are afraid of towels because they are associated with something unpleasant. You can make a towel fun, or at least less threatening, by encouraging your Eclectus to play on or under one while you snuggle with him.

The sound of running tap water encourages this Eclectus to splash happily on a wet countertop. Some birds prefer bathing in the gentle mist from a spray bottle while others enjoy showering with their owners.

New, still growing blood feathers are not as easily visible in an Eclectus as they are in the wing of this white cockatoo. When the feathers reach their full length, the blood will recede and it will again be safe to trim them.

This Solomon Islands Eclectus female is undergoing a natural feather molt to replace old, worn plumage. Note the missing feathers that expose the gray down beneath.

Trimming Flight Feathers

Eclectus parrots are heavy-bodied birds that usually require a less severe clip than other parrots. If the bird falls and hurts itself repeatedly because its wings were clipped too short, it will have a dramatic effect on its sense of well-being and its inclination toward vigorous exercise or rowdy play. There is no excuse for cutting wings back so severely that the bird can no longer land softly, but veterinarians and animal groomers with little avian experience are often the worst offenders. It is important that everyone involved understands what a wing trim is suppose to accomplish. *A proper wing clip that will allow a bird to play confidently indoors may also allow it to become airborne outdoors under certain conditions. It is the owner's responsibility to see that the parrot is always in a cage or carrier when it is taken outdoors!*

Many experienced avian veterinarians feel that severe wing trims are a probable cause of feather chewing and plucking in sensitive parrots such as Eclectus. This could be due to stress or fear caused by poor coordination and balance skills, or the discomfort of being continually poked in the side

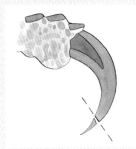

Only the sharp tip of a parrot's toenail should be trimmed. If a nail bleeds, pack the end with cornstarch or flour.

by the short, sharp ends of clipped feather quills.

Method

While many parrot owners leave wing clipping to their veterinarian during the bird's annual checkup, it is safer and less stressful for an Eclectus if the owner learns to do a gradual progressive clip, and then keeps each flight feather trimmed back as it grows in. In a progressive clip, two or three of the outermost primary flight feathers on each wing tip are clipped back, leaving about one and one-half inches extending from beneath the overlying covert feathers. Then the bird is watched for two or three days to see how its flight and attitude are affected. Every few days one more feather on each wing is trimmed back until the bird decides that flying more than

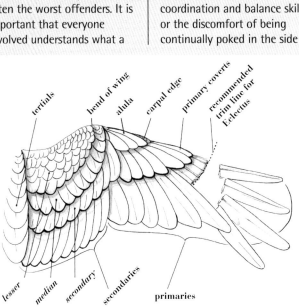

Flight feathers should be trimmed back one at a time until the desired effect is achieved. An Eclectus must be able to glide safely to the floor.

a few feet is more trouble than it is worth. Always clip the same number of feathers on each wing so that the bird is balanced.

By using this method, only enough feathers are removed to achieve the desired effect. In the months ahead, as the clipped flight feathers are gradually molted one by one, each new feather that grows in is allowed to develop past the blood feather stage and then is trimmed back to the same height as its neighbors. Because this method entails clipping only one or two feathers at a time, it can often be done without restraining the bird.

What Are Blood Feathers?

Feathers are essential for flight, insulation, and waterproofing. Once or twice a year the old feather, whether clipped or not, is pushed out when a new feather begins growing in its place. For the short time it takes a new feather to grow to maturity, it is alive and sensitive and your Eclectus will probably object to it being touched. If the bird is growing several big, new flight feathers or tail feathers at once it might be irritable and nippy. If you look closely at the underside of your bird's wing where the feathers meet the skin, a new feather shaft will appear soft, swollen, and full of blood—rather like a drinking straw full of tomato juice. This is a blood feather. Because it is connected directly to a blood source in the wing, it will bleed if accidentally cut or broken. As soon as the feather reaches its full length, the blood will recede and the shaft will shrink, harden, and lose all sensitivity. At this point the feather is again safe to clip.

Trimming Toenails and Beaks

The use of textured cement perches to keep the tips of your pet Eclectus' razor-sharp toenails rounded off is highly recommended and reduces the need for regular trimming. If these perches are to do a good job, it is important to get the diameter that the manufacturer recommends for Eclectus-size birds.

If you find it necessary to trim your Eclectus' sharp toenails to make holding it more comfortable, clip only the very tip with a pair of sharp fingernail clippers or a pair of curved nail scissors intended for small animals. A coarse emery board designed for women's acrylic nails also works well. Never cut nails back to the sensitive quick. If they are very long it is best to trim them back gradually or have your veterinarian do it. If a clipped nail begins to bleed, pack cornstarch or flour into the cut end. Several applications may be necessary. Toenail trimming should be done with the bird's needs in mind. Eclectus have small feet for their body size and need their nails to securely grip their perches, especially if their wings have been clipped.

A parrot's beak contains highly sensitive nerve endings and should never be subjected to routine cosmetic filing or trimming. An overgrown beak is unusual in a healthy parrot and may indicate disease or dietary problems. If filing or reshaping a parrot's beak is necessary, it should always be done by a veterinarian. Normal wear of your Eclectus' beak should be encouraged by offering the bird plenty of soft wood toys and fresh green twigs or branches to chew.

Scissors with curved cutting edges are suitable for trimming both toenails and flight feathers. Coarse emery boards designed for women's acrylic nails are useful for rounding off sharp nail tips between trims.

KEEPING YOUR ECLECTUS HEALTHY

Learning to be observant of your Eclectus' behavior, weighing it weekly, and finding a veterinarian with an interest in birds will go a long way toward keeping your parrot healthy.

Preventing Illness

Hiding Illness

Most people assume that birds are more delicate than dogs and cats because it seems everyone has memories of a pet parrot that looked good one day and was dead the next! Well-cared-for parrots are usually remarkably hardy and long-lived. In the wild, however, they are prey animals with deeply ingrained defense mechanisms. A sick or injured Eclectus parrot instinctively knows that it will attract predators or be driven away by members of its own flock, so it will go to desperate lengths to behave normally for as long as possible. Pet parrots are also good at hiding weakness, and an owner often misses the subtle signs of illness until the bird is unable to hide them any longer.

There are several easy ways to keep your Eclectus healthy and free of disease:

A Red-sided Eclectus male and female (E. roratus polychloros) from New Guinea and the western Papuan Islands.

1. Know your bird. Be observant of your bird's normal appearance, behavior, and habits now so that you will recognize subtle changes. Be aware of when your Eclectus normally awakens, eats, plays, naps, and goes to sleep for the night. Know how much food and water it consumes each day. Any change in activity, appearance, voice, or personality should alert a watchful owner. All sick birds share basic symptoms regardless of the cause. Their feathers will be fluffed in an effort to conserve heat, they will vocalize less, and will look sleepy when they would normally be active. Some parrots will drop their guard only when they think no one is watching. A very sick bird may continue eating and drinking but might become unusually picky about what it eats. Eclectus are such enthusiastic eaters that any lack of interest in food should cause concern. Always check the cage papers daily before throwing them out. A change in color, consistency, or number of droppings should be noted.

2. Perform routine weight checks. Purchase an accurate gram scale and weigh your Eclectus

once a week, preferably at the same time of day. A sick bird can't properly utilize the food it eats and usually begins to lose weight. A sudden unexplained weight loss may well be an owner's first clue that something is wrong. Scales are available with built-in perches to make weighing birds easy and accurate. They are available from cage bird supply catalogs or your veterinarian will be able to recommend a supplier. A scale that weighs in ounces or one intended to weigh food portions will not be accurate enough. If you don't have a scale, make a point of feeling the keel or breastbone regularly. If the bird begins to lose weight the pectoral muscles on either side of the sternum will shrink, leaving the keel feeling sharp and pointy.

3. Have annual checkups. Have your Eclectus examined annually by a competent avian veterinarian. Don't wait for an emergency to look for an avian veterinarian. Contact local pet shops, breeders, and bird clubs for recommendations, then schedule your Eclectus for a well-bird exam. A veterinarian experienced with parrots will not have to run a battery of expensive tests each year if a bird appears healthy and is acting normally.

4. Stay away from other birds. Parrots contract disease from other parrots. Don't allow your bird to come in contact with unknown parrots or things they have touched. If you visit a bird store or bird fair where parrots are sold, shower and change clothes before handling your Eclectus. If you buy toys or other items that are not sealed in plastic from a place that handles live parrots, scrub them with soap and hot water before giving them to your bird.

5. Quarantine new birds. If you already have parrots, a new bird, regardless of its origin, should be checked by your veterinarian and then be isolated and quarantined in another room away from your other birds for at least a month. A quarantined bird should always be fed and handled after tending to the others, and you should wash your hands carefully afterward. It is a good idea to keep a long-sleeved shirt or smock in the quarantine room that you wear only when handling the new bird. Watch the new bird closely for signs of illness.

Recognizing Illness

Birds instinctively hide sickness for as long as they can. An Eclectus that is fluffed, sleepy-looking, and unusually quiet for long periods, or one that is unsteady, having difficulty breathing, or, worse yet, sitting on the bottom of its cage, may have been ill for some time. It should be kept warm and be seen by your veterinarian immediately as an emergency. Do not offer food or water just prior to an exam; the bird could aspirate while being examined.

The following symptoms are serious warning signs that should be investigated by your veterinarian as soon as possible:

✔ Sudden unexplained weight loss is often the first sign of illness. A gram scale is a valuable part of a first aid kit and should be used weekly.

✔ A change in the tone or volume of voice, audible breathing, or an odd clicking sound when the bird breathes can indicate respiratory problems. A bird working hard to breathe may dip its tail with each breath.

✔ Persistent wet or stained feathers around the nostrils or crusty material in and around the nostrils could indicate respiratory problems. Birds have a highly efficient respiratory system and are susceptible to intoxication and irritation from smoking, airborne particles, and gases. The cause should be investigated because chronic upper respiratory disease can be difficult to cure.

✔ A puffy, swollen area around one or both eyes, drainage from the eyes, redness of the eyes or surrounding areas, or feather loss around the eyes indicates possible sinus or respiratory infection.

✔ Breathing that takes a long time to return to normal after exercise or an examination.

✔ Changes in personality or behavior that can't be explained by molting, adolescence, or changes in household routine should always be noted. Parrots are supposed to be noisy and demanding. A chatterbox that stops talking or vocalizing may not be feeling well. The same is true for a gentle bird that becomes grumpy or a nippy one that suddenly tolerates touching.

✔ A very ill bird will often continue to eat but may become unusually picky—perhaps refusing all but one or two favorite food items.

✔ Vomiting, or expelling food from the stomach or proventriculus, and regurgitation, which occurs when food is brought up from the crop, both indicate possible gastrointestinal problems and can result in rapid weight loss from dehydration. Keep in mind that regurgitation is normal behavior for a male Eclectus that attempts to feed a favorite person as he would a mate.

✔ Droppings do not adhere to the vent feathers of a healthy bird. A dirty, pasty vent is a sign of gastrointestinal problems.

✔ Swellings can be ruptured air sacs or tumors and should be seen by a veterinarian as soon as possible.

✔ Lameness can be due to sore feet caused by unsuitable perches, poor nutrition, or bacterial infections, and can become serious if not addressed. Leg injuries result from falls when wings are clipped too short. Abdominal tumors sometimes cause lameness.

✔ Overgrown beak and toenails can indicate disease or nutritional problems. Eclectus should always have plenty of soft wood to chew to keep their beaks in good condition.

✔ Feather color and condition are a good indication of an Eclectus parrot's emotional and physical health, and any changes should be brought to your veterinarian's attention. A bird that molts continuously or whose feathers appear misshapen as they emerge from the skin could be suffering from disease. Feathers with yellow or orange markings, black splotches, or a greasy appearance, indicate poor nutrition. A bird with normal head feathers but scruffy, worn-out, or missing plumage below its neck is abusing its feathers. The reasons for feather picking in Eclectus parrots are not well understood, but the behavior can be triggered by prolonged fear, stress, pain, discomfort, health problems, and poor nutrition. It can eventually become habit, so the cause should be investigated.

✔ Feathers require a great deal of maintenance and healthy parrots spend a good part of each day preening and grooming their feathers to keep them in good condition. Absence of preening is an indication that something is wrong.

✔ Repetitive, involuntary toe tapping or foot clenching, often accompanied by wing flipping, is a puzzling syndrome apparently seen only in Eclectus parrots. It seems to be triggered by nutritional factors that may differ from bird to bird, such as oversupplementing vitamins and minerals or low blood calcium levels. Incidents

The first symptom of illness is often weight loss. Purchase an accurate gram scale and weigh your Eclectus once a week.

often last a week or more and may or may not reappear. More studies are needed to better understand this problem. It is not considered an emergency but should be called to your veterinarian's attention.

Evaluating Your Bird's Droppings

The color, consistency, frequency, and volume of a bird's droppings are a clue to its health. Know what your bird's normal droppings look like after it has been eating various foods. Use paper on the cage bottom and take time to check the appearance and amount of droppings daily.

A dropping consists of three parts: the *feces,* the *urates,* and the *urine.* The feces are the dark, solid part that consists of food waste from the digestive tract. They can vary in color and consistency depending on the diet. Well-formed, tubular, dark green feces are usually produced by birds on seed diets. Birds that are fed pellets produce soft, loose brownish feces, while those from a parrot that has eaten beets, berries, or treats containing food dyes may be brightly colored. The urates are the creamy white portion of the dropping peculiar to birds, reptiles, and amphibians. They are a waste product of the kidneys and often appear suspended in the urine or wrapped around the feces. The urine is the clear, colorless liquid that surrounds the dropping. The amount of urine in the dropping depends on the bird's water consumption (including moisture from fruits and vegetables), as well as its emotional state. All of the body wastes collect in a single area called the *cloaca,* which means sewer in Latin. The external opening of the cloaca is the *vent.*

Abnormal Droppings

The following changes in a parrot's droppings should be monitored and your veterinarian should be contacted if they continue for more than a few days:

Appearance	Possible Reason
Urates yellowish or greenish in color instead of cream or white.	Indicates illness such as liver disease.
Urine greenish in color instead of clear.	May indicate liver disease.
Increased urination with properly formed stools.	This is *polyuria*, not diarrhea, and is usually a sign of increased water consumption. A bird that eats lots of fruits and vegetables will naturally produce more urine, but one that consistently drinks more water than seems normal could have diabetes or liver problems. It is normal for an excited or frightened bird to produce droppings that are mostly urine.
Odorous droppings.	Fresh droppings have little or no odor. A change in smell should be brought to your veterinarian's attention.
Blood in any part of the droppings.	Blood in the droppings may indicate heavy metal poisoning or other serious problems. The bird should be evaluated immediately by a veterinarian. **Note:** Owners have been fooled by colored dyes in the bird's food or colored ink in the cage papers that can cause the appearance of bloody droppings.
Scant, black, sticky droppings.	Usually means that a bird has not eaten in at least 24 hours and should be seen by a veterinarian as soon as possible.
Foamy, bubbly droppings.	May indicate gas formed by certain kinds of bacteria.
Feces have a runny consistency.	Diarrhea is an increase in the water content of the feces and could indicate gastrointestinal tract infection or intestinal parasites.
Passing whole seed in the droppings.	May be a symptom of disease or intestinal parasites.
A pile of droppings in one place.	May be an indication that the bird is not as active as usual. Owner should increase observation to be certain all is well.
A decrease in the total number of droppings.	The bird may be eating less. Owner should increase observation.

Dealing with Emergencies

Heat, food and liquids, and minimal stress are the most important requirements of a sick or injured bird, both before it is seen by a veterinarian and during its recovery.

Heat: Keep the bird quiet and maintain a temperature of 85°F (29°C). A temporary hospital cage can be made by placing a heating pad under one end of a carrier, box, small cage, or aquarium, and covering it with a blanket. If the bird is able to perch, you can drape blankets around the sides of its cage and hang a ceramic heating element designed especially for birds and reptiles or a 100-watt lightbulb over it. A ceramic heater is preferable because it does not give off light and will allow a sick bird to sleep. It screws into an ordinary incandescent lamp socket. Do not use a heat source that can create fumes, such as a kerosene heater. The temperature should be monitored constantly. *Be sure that the bird can move away from the heat source if necessary.* If it pants and holds its wings away from its body, the temperature is too high. If the bird cannot perch, cover the bottom of the box or carrier with towels for traction. A hot water bottle wrapped in a towel will supply warmth for the trip to the veterinarian.

Food and liquids: Every effort must be made to encourage a sick bird to eat and drink. Make sure that its favorite foods are within easy reach and offer them often, by hand if necessary. Make sure fresh water is available and offer warm fruit juice, Pedialyte, or other liquid by dropper or spoon to help prevent dehydration. A bird that was hand-fed as a baby will often take warm hand-feeding formula or other soft, hot, mashed foods from a spoon or syringe. Do not offer your bird food or water just prior to taking it to the veterinarian because it could vomit and aspirate during the examination.

Peace and quiet: Stress reduction is important when managing a sick bird. Keep it in a warm, quiet place and handle or disturb only when necessary.

Emergency Procedures

Bites and scratches: A bite or scratch from a cat, dog, or wild animal can cause a fatal septicemia with *Pasteurella* bacteria within 24 hours, even if the wound itself doesn't seem serious. Clean with hydrogen peroxide or soap and water, or flush with water if near an eye. The bird should receive antibiotic treatment by a veterinarian immediately.

CHECKLIST

What NOT to Do

1 Do not administer medicines, antibiotics, alcohol, or oil of any kind unless instructed by your veterinarian.
2 If it is necessary to restrain your Eclectus in a towel for emergency treatment, be careful not to impede its breathing by putting pressure on its chest.
3 Do not apply flour or cornstarch to a skin laceration or feather follicle. Use it only to stop bleeding from a broken feather shaft, cracked or broken beak, or broken toenail.
4 Never apply greasy ointments. They will spread to the feathers, destroying their thermal efficiency.

Fractures: A bird that allows its wing to droop or refuses to put weight on a leg should be seen by a veterinarian as soon as possible. If the bird is active and likely to cause further damage to a broken wing, support it by using a self-adherent bandage such as Vetrap to tape the wing to its body. (Vetrap bandage sticks only to itself, not to the bird's feathers.) Masking tape can be used in a pinch and will cause minimal damage to feathers. Be careful that the bandage isn't tight enough to impede breathing.

Bleeding lacerations and broken toenails: Several minutes of steady pressure may be required before the bleeding slows. Use hydrogen peroxide to wet the feathers and help determine the source of bleeding. Press cornstarch or flour into the end of a bleeding beak or toenail while applying pressure. Sometimes an ice cube pressed into the end of a bleeding nail will help.

Broken blood feathers: Large, new blood feathers in the wings and tail are connected to a blood source beneath the skin and will bleed if broken or damaged. Try packing the open end of the feather shaft with cornstarch or flour. Several applications may be needed, but in most cases the bleeding will eventually stop. *Don't panic.* It may help to remember that it is extremely unusual for a bird the size of an Eclectus to bleed to death from a broken blood feather. If the bleeding doesn't stop, the feather will have to be pulled. This procedure can be painful and is best done by your veterinarian, veterinary technician, or an experienced bird owner. If you can't get to a veterinarian, you will need someone to help you. Wrap the bird in a bath towel with its face covered, being careful not to put pressure on its chest. Support the wing or base of the

CHECKLIST

First Aid Kit
- ✔ Gram scale
- ✔ Hemostats or needlenosed pliers
- ✔ Self-adherent bandage such as Vetrap
- ✔ Cotton gauze pads
- ✔ Peroxide
- ✔ Plastic eyedroppers or syringes without needles for administering fluids
- ✔ Spoon with the sides bent up
- ✔ KY jelly for an egg-bound hen
- ✔ Cornstarch or flour
- ✔ Heating pad or ceramic heating element
- ✔ Small cage, carrier, or aquarium suitable for use as a hospital cage
- ✔ Portable cage or carrier with cover and food and water dishes for each bird in your home in case of emergency evacuation because of toxic household fumes, fire, tornado, hurricane, and so on
- ✔ Aloe vera plant. The fresh gel is useful for minor cuts, burns, and abrasions and is thought to be superior to products containing aloe.

tail close to the base of the bleeding feather with one hand to prevent breaking any bones, and use a pair of hemostats or needlenosed pliers to firmly grasp the feather as close to the skin as possible. Pull the feather straight out in the direction of growth. The bird may scream, so don't be startled. Examine the end of the feather shaft to be certain it is all there. If a remnant of feather shaft is left in the skin,

A first aid kit should be kept on hand for emergencies. From left to right are hemostats, a bent spoon, cotton gauze, Vetrap bandage, an aloe vera plant, a ceramic heating element, corn starch, KY Jelly, syringes without needles, and an eyedropper.

it will need to be pulled out or the bleeding will continue. Apply gentle pressure to the skin until the bleeding stops. Do not apply flour, cornstarch, blood stop powder, or ointment to the bird's skin.

Finding an Avian Veterinarian

Until recently, parrot owners often found it difficult to locate a veterinarian who had experience with birds. The subject of pet birds was not addressed in veterinary schools, little diagnostic screening for disease was available, and even less was known about drug dosage regimens. Today we have veterinarians and researchers who deal exclusively with birds. Our technology is improving rapidly and avian veterinarians, breeders, and owners are looking forward to the time when there will be tests and vaccines to control the most serious diseases and our main concern will be managing the metabolic ailments of our aging pets. For now, though, avian medicine still lags behind our knowledge of dogs, cats, and other domestic animals, and it is important to

find a veterinarian who is genuinely interested in birds and makes an effort to keep up with the latest research.

The Association of Avian Veterinarians (AAV) offers continuing education classes at major conferences and is an excellent resource for veterinarians interested in treating birds. The AAV maintains a current membership list and is a good way of tracking down an Avian Veterinarian close to you (see Information, page 92, for address). Bird magazines often have listings for Avian Veterinarians. Local bird clubs, bird breeders, and pet shops are also good sources of information.

If possible, choose a veterinarian who has the facilities and experience to do avian in-house diagnostic testing. A sick bird may not have time to wait for test results from a distant laboratory. Ask how the veterinarian handles after-hours emergencies; a competent veterinarian is of little value if he or she isn't available when your bird is sick or injured.

The Avian Exam

What to Expect

New bird owners are often surprised to discover how expensive avian veterinary care can be. Sick birds usually exhibit similar outward symptoms regardless of what illness they are suffering. An accurate diagnosis often depends on lab work, radiographs, and endoscopy, none of which are cheap. This is all the more reason to catch potential problems early by having a basic well-bird exam done once a year.

Nervous birds tend to produce droppings that are mostly urine. Remember to put clean newspaper or freezer paper on the cage bottom a few hours before the scheduled exam so that a few typical droppings can be collected and taken along.

Which tests your veterinarian feels are important will depend on the age and origin of the bird, the prevalence of disease in your area, and the result of an external exam, complete blood count (CBC), and Gram stains. The reason for each additional diagnostic procedure should be explained and its cost should be discussed openly beforehand.

The initial new-bird exam will be more extensive than the yearly routine checks that follow and should establish a baseline for comparison. It will include taking a full history, a thorough external physical exam, and weight recording along with some *(not all)* of the diagnostic tests listed below.

Routine (Annual) Tests

✔ Complete blood count (CBC): A good indicator of a bird's general health and the single

The appearance of odd red, orange, or yellow feathers may indicate illness such as liver disease or dietary problems. This young male developed a temporary sprinkling of colored feathers on his chest after undergoing back-to-back antibiotic regimens for an injured foot and an ear infection.

most important test your veterinarian will perform. It identifies cells that are involved in the inflammatory and disease-fighting processes and determines if the bird is anemic. A CBC should be part of your Eclectus' annual exam.

Note: Eclectus parrots are well known for exhibiting temporary, stress-induced elevated white blood cell counts during examinations. A veterinarian who doesn't see many Eclectus might mistake this increase in white cells for evidence of a bacterial or viral infection.

✔ Fecal Gram stains: Swabs of feces that are smeared on slides, then stained and examined under the microscope. The Gram stain is a quick, inexpensive method of evaluating the microbial status of the digestive tract and should be done annually.

✔ Examination of droppings: For example, urates that are green or yellow instead of creamy white suggest the possibility of liver damage and would be reason to do further testing.

Exploratory or Baseline Tests

✔ Plasma or serum chemistry panel: A group of 5 to 15 tests that measure various chemicals in blood plasma to assess organ damage, kidney function, and low blood sugar or low calcium levels.

✔ Cultures: Material collected from the cloaca and/or choana (back of the throat) that is grown in the laboratory to test for abnormal bacteria and fungi. Growing or "culturing" microorganisms is the only way to positively identify them and determine what drugs they are sensitive to.

✔ Urinalysis: Test that is useful in birds that are producing excessive urine to check for diabetes or kidney damage.

✔ Fecal parasite check: Microscopic examination of droppings to detect parasites or their eggs; especially important in birds that have been housed outdoors in southern states.

✔ Radiographs (X-rays): Tests that are useful to investigate trauma and to look for changes in internal organs.

✔ Endoscopy: A valuable technique for visualizing the internal organs by introducing a fiber-optic telescope through a tiny incision while the bird is anesthetized. The scope can also be used to examine the respiratory tract and to collect biopsy specimens.

✔ Ultrasound: A sound picture of internal organs that is especially useful for assessing abnormal internal masses.

Tests for Specific Diseases

Tests are available for diseases that are difficult to identify from the above procedures.

Disease testing is routinely done on new birds to prevent exposure to existing pets.

✔ Psittacine beak and feather disease testing (PBFD): A highly contagious viral disease that causes abnormal beak and feather growth and suppression of the immune system. It is seen most often in Asian and Australian psittacines. Eclectus parrots usually do not show involvement of the beak. It is highly recommended that every new parrot be tested for PBFD before it comes in contact with established pet birds. It is important to understand that a positive test result may mean that the bird was recently exposed to the disease and is in the process of successfully eliminating the virus from its body. A second test should be done in 90 days to determine if there is an infection. There is no treatment and an infection is always fatal.

✔ Polyomavirus disease testing: Polyoma is a viral disease that can spread rapidly through a breeder's nursery killing baby parrots that are still being hand-fed. Young Eclectus seem to be particularly susceptible to polyoma and may be at risk up to 14 months old. It is rarely fatal in adult birds and most make a complete recovery. A DNA test is available for polyoma. A vaccine is currently being marketed, but there is some disagreement as to its effectiveness.

✔ Aspergillosis disease testing: Aspergillosis is a fungal infection that usually affects the respiratory system. Aspergillum spores thrive in dampness and are common in the environment. When inhaled by a bird whose resistance is low, they can begin growing in lungs and air sacs. The disease is treatable in its early stages, but advanced cases have a poor prognosis. Eclectus seem particularly susceptible to aspergillosis and it is especially common in breeding hens that spend most of the time in their nest boxes. Any changes in an Eclectus' breathing or the pitch of its voice should be suspect. It is not contagious.

✔ Chlamydiosis disease testing: Also known as psittacosis or parrot fever, Chlamydia is a bacterial infection that can be serious if not treated. It can be transmitted to humans from many species of birds, including doves, pigeons, birds of prey, shore birds, and parrots. Budgerigars (parakeets) and cockatiels are common sources of outbreaks in larger parrots and people because they are capable of carrying the disease without showing symptoms. The disease responds well to antibiotic treatment in both birds and people. There is no vaccine at present.

Note: Symptoms in humans resemble an abrupt onset of influenza or other respiratory illness.

✔ Pacheco's disease testing: Also known as the psittacine herpes virus, Pacheco's virus attacks the liver and can cause sudden death in pet and aviary birds of all ages. Immediate treatment may prevent infection in some birds in a collection if the virus is identified quickly enough. A bird that manages to survive an infection—most often conures and amazons—is likely to carry the disease for the rest of its life and expose other parrots it comes in contact with. If Pacheco's is common in your area and you have one of these species of parrots, your veterinarian may suggest having it tested before bringing your new Eclectus home. A vaccine is available but its safety is somewhat controversial. It will protect your parrot from contracting the disease but will not prevent it from transmitting the infection to other susceptible birds.

✔ Proventricular Dilatation Disease (PDD): Formerly known as macaw wasting disease, most parrot species including many wild birds and waterfowl can be affected. Clinical signs include progressive weight loss, passage of whole seeds in the droppings, regurgitation, and enlargement of the proventriculus, or stomach. There is a neurological form of the disease in which the bird appears unsteady and may have difficulty perching. The incubation period may last several months or years, during which time infected birds appear healthy but can transmit the virus to other parrots. An accurate diagnosis is difficult to obtain in a live bird and an infection is always fatal. Researchers are presently working to develop a test for PDD.

When a Bird Dies

It is often difficult for an owner to deal with having a necropsy, or animal autopsy, performed to determine the cause of death of a cherished pet. It is necessary, however, to protect the health and safety of remaining birds in the home and the knowledge will be invaluable when a new bird is added to the family. When a bird dies, it is important to cool the body as quickly as possible. Soak it in cold, soapy water, which will quickly penetrate feathers and release trapped body heat. Wrap the bird in a plastic bag and keep it refrigerated, *not frozen*, until it can be taken to a veterinarian.

MAKING YOUR HOME SAFE FOR YOUR ECLECTUS

Birds are more sensitive than people to toxins in the environment. Fumes from nonstick cookware, self-cleaning ovens, and air fresheners and cleaning products are especially dangerous.

Possible Dangers

A pet parrot whose wings have been clipped is likely to have poor flying skills if its flight feathers are accidentally permitted to grow back. When startled, it may sustain a concussion or broken beak by flying into ceiling fans, mirrors, or windows. If you have made the decision to clip your Eclectus' wings, check often for growing flight feathers and keep them trimmed back so that the bird can land gently on the floor but cannot gain altitude. Keep your bird safely in its cage while you are using the stovetop, oven, or other dangerous appliances.

An Eclectus should never be out of its cage without adult supervision. It can drown in the toilet, sink, or bathtub, or hang itself in the cords from roll-up shades and blinds. All parrots seem to delight in seeking out and chewing on electric cords. They are often stepped

A Red-sided Eclectus female (E. roratus polychloros).

or sat on by children and scratched or bitten by cats, dogs, and other parrots.

Birds have a highly efficient respiratory system and are more prone than humans to intoxication and irritation from smoking, airborne particles, and gases. They often chew on household items that were never intended for ingestion and are commonly treated for zinc and lead poisoning. Some substances that have been linked to avian deaths are listed below. Most homes contain many other products that could be toxic if inhaled or ingested. Read the label; if it isn't good for you, it's doubly bad for your Eclectus.

Airborne Toxins

Nonstick Coatings: Toxic fumes from overheated polytetrafluoroethylene (PTFE)-coated cookware such as Teflon, Silverstone, and Supra will quickly kill a bird. The introduction of a pet Eclectus to a household is an excellent reason to purchase new, safe, uncoated cookware!

Also dangerous are items such as PTFE-coated drip pans, burner pans, and grill plates that are routinely heated to 530°F (250°C)—the point at which the coating begins to break down and give off a deadly odorless gas. Unfortunately, consumers may have to guess which products have PTFE coatings because in many instances they are not listed. Bird owners should be especially careful with irons, ironing board covers, waffle irons, hair dryers, heat lamps, and space heaters, which often have PTFE-coated parts. These products should be used only in well-ventilated areas away from pet birds.

New heaters and appliances: Most metal parts are factory sprayed with protective finishes that burn off the first time they are used. Be certain to open all doors and windows and turn on exhaust fans, or better yet, remove all birds prior to heating any new metal surface for the first time.

Self-cleaning ovens: The fumes have caused the death of pet parrots even though the birds were not in the kitchen at the time.

Aerosol sprays: The fluorocarbon propellant in all aerosol sprays is toxic to birds even if the product in the can is not.

Cleaners, deodorizers, and other household products: Fumes from air fresheners, room and carpet deodorants, suede waterproofing sprays, chlorine bleach, ammonia, drain openers, insecticides, paints, paint thinners, and glue are all toxic to varying degrees and may have cumulative effects if the bird is exposed often.

Carbon monoxide (CO) fumes and natural gas leaks: The fumes can cause serious injury or death to birds before being noticed by people.

Tobacco smoke: Birds from households where there are heavy smokers often suffer from respiratory problems and feather plucking. Nicotine residue on smokers' hands can cause dermatitis on the bird's feet.

Ingested Toxins

Foods: Foods known to be harmful to birds include alcohol, avocados, chocolate, and anything containing caffeine. Peanuts are best avoided because they often harbor invisible *mycotoxins* that can remain long after the fungus that produced them has died. Foods that are dusty, damaged by insects, have molds present, or don't smell fresh should not be offered to birds.

Zinc and lead: Avian veterinarians have only recently discovered that zinc and lead toxicity in pet birds is far more common and serious than once believed. Zinc or lead is often present in galvanized food and water dishes, pennies, costume jewelry, some wine bottle foil, leaded glass, bells with lead clappers, some paints and powder coatings, flooring and flooring adhesives, tire balances, curtain weights, fishing sinkers, galvanized wire, twist ties, duct tape, and many other household items. Examine your Eclectus' toys often and replace any metal chains, hooks, quick links, and bells that peel, flake, or show a powdery white corrosion. Symptoms of zinc or lead toxicity can surface quickly or over a long period of time depending on the amount ingested. They may include lethargy, depression, weakness, vomiting, refusal to eat, voluminous green droppings, seizures or poor coordination, bloody droppings, and feather plucking. Blood tests are readily available to determine whether a bird's zinc and lead levels are within a safe range. *Chelation agents*—drugs that chemically bind to the metal and remove it from the bloodstream are effective if administered early.

Cage substrates: Avoid corncob, crushed walnut shell, and kitty litter in cage bottoms and playstands. When ingested these materials can swell, causing blockage of the ventriculus or gizzard.

Plants: There is a long list of plants and trees of known toxicity to mammals, but few documented cases of plant poisonings in birds. In fact, many of the plants that birds feed upon in the wild are reported to be toxic to either humans or livestock. It is speculated that their rapid gastrointestinal transit time might eliminate ingested plant material before high levels of toxins can be absorbed. *Avocados are a notable exception and all parts of the fruit and plant are best avoided.* Eclectus enjoy chewing on soft, fresh green twigs and this is a wonderful way to keep them occupied. Avoid trees grown in orchards or along roadsides where pesticides are sprayed.

Other toxic household items: Matches, tobacco, styptic pencils, pencils, and pelleted fertilizers can be harmful if ingested.

Safe Plants and Trees

Acacia	Corn Plant	Hen and Chickens	Pear
African Violet	Cottonwood	Hibiscus	Pepperomia
Aloe vera	Crab Apple	Honey locust	Petunia
Apple	Dandelion	Huckleberry	Poplar
Arbutus	Dogwood	Jade Plant	Prayer Plant
Ash	Donkey Tail	Kalanchoe	Prune
Aspen	Dracaena varieties	Larch	Purple Passion (velvet
Autumn Olive	Elm	Lavender	nettle)
Baby Tears	Eucalyptus	Magnolia	Quince
Bamboo	Ferns (asparagus,	Marigold	Ribbonwood
Bee Balm	bird's nest, Boston,	Monkey Plant	Sassafras
Beech	maidenhair)	Mulberry	Sensitive Plant
Begonia	Figs (creeping, rubber,	Nasturtium	Sequoia (Redwood)
Birch	fiddle leaf, laurel	Natal Plum	Spider Plant
Bougainvillea	leaf, weeping)	Norfolk Island Pine	Spruce
Butterfly bush	Fir	Nut (except chestnut	Swedish Ivy
Chickweed	Forsythia	and oak)	Thistle
Christmas cactus	Gardenia	Palms (areca, date,	Wandering Jew
Citrus	Grape Ivy	fan, lady, parlour,	Wax Plant
Coleus	Grape Vine	howela, kentia,	White Clover
Comfrey	Guava	sago, phoenix)	Willow
Coneflower	Hawthorn	Papaya	Zebra Plant

LIVING WITH YOUR ECLECTUS PARROT

"Parrots reflect our energy and mood, and can teach us a great deal about ourselves— if we pay attention."

—*Sally Blanchard*
author and behaviorist

The First Few Days

The first few days in its new home will be less stressful for your Eclectus if you handle it as little as possible. The bird needs time to become accustomed to its new cage, surroundings, and family members and pets without feeling frightened or overwhelmed. Offer him whatever brand of pellets or seed he is familiar with; there will be plenty of time later to make changes. Take turns sitting beside the cage talking quietly to him; he will find you less intimidating if you are not towering above him. If there are children in the family, have them read storybooks aloud. The bird will find the sound soothing. With your fingers, offer warm kernels of sweet corn or other familiar food through the cage bars. A shy bird will come around much faster if you limit direct eye contact. Staring is something predators do; it's never polite, and for all he knows you are planning to have him for dinner!

Sounds such as the hum of a vacuum cleaner often motivate Eclectus parrots to bathe.

Keep in mind that unlike most parrots, Eclectus mask stress and worry by putting on a calm, quiet front. When he begins to move about the cage and show an interest in his food and toys, you will know that he is ready to begin interacting with family members outside the cage.

Establishing Boundaries

A baby parrot is born without the foggiest idea how to be a good pet. Your baby Eclectus will be all grown up in a few short years, and *you* are directly responsible for teaching it the skills it will need to successfully and happily coexist with people for the rest of its life. When you are certain that your Eclectus feels safe and happy in its new environment, it is time to begin setting the clearly defined physical and behavioral boundaries, or rules, that will ensure that it remains a valued family member.

Commands

Using Sally Blanchard's techniques of Nurturing Guidance, the bird is taught the verbal commands *"Up"* and *"Down"* until the patterned response is reliable and *completely automatic*. Always use the *"Up"* command when you are asking a parrot to step onto your hand and the *"Down"* command when it is stepping off your hand. Begin by gently pressing your fingers into your Eclectus' lower belly as you say *"Up."* A young bird may test the security of your hand with its beak before stepping up and it is important not to pull away. Your voice should be firm but friendly and quiet, and your manner gentle. Don't forget to smile! These training sessions should be short, upbeat, and accompanied by enthusiastic praise when the parrot complies. There must be no doubt that the bird understands when it has done something correctly. This is a simple, positive first step toward better communication and a trusting relationship between you and your Eclectus.

Stick Training

When your Eclectus is responding automatically to the *"Up"* and *"Down"* commands, teach it to do the same from a wooden dowel or perch that you hold in your hand. If you ever have to handle your bird when it has become territorial or overstimulated, having it "stick trained" will keep you in control and prevent a bite. Parrots clearly respect and enjoy being around people who set reasonable, easy-to-understand behavior limits, and they will often go out of their way to intimidate those who do not. Behavior experts often remind us that lack of control by the owner is the most common source of behavior problems in parrots. If a young bird is allowed to do anything it pleases, it may become difficult to handle as it matures. Your parrot will readily accept you as the one in charge, but like a small child it will

sometimes feel the need to test authority. If you use the *"Up"* and *"Down"* commands consistently throughout its life, the bird will be gently reminded every day that you are in charge and it will always have something that it can do to earn your praise.

Limiting Freedom

It is important for an Eclectus to spend time out of its cage, but you are not doing your bird a favor by allowing it unlimited freedom. As parrots mature, they sometimes exhibit aggressive territorial behavior around their cages, and a bird that can come and go as it pleases may attempt to expand its territory. An Eclectus should view its cage as its castle—a place of security, comfort, and freedom, where it is permitted to chew wood, fling food, beat up toys, play, relax, sleep, and do as it pleases. A cage should be as large as possible and filled with toys that are rotated regularly.

Respecting Your Bird's Feelings

Avian conservationists and biologists who spend hours in the field observing flocks of wild parrots tell us that they rarely see aggressive physical confrontations between flock members. Parrots use body language to communicate, and the confidant swagger of a mature, wily, male parrot is unmistakable to another bird. A young Eclectus learns quickly that raised hackles and flashing eyes mean that it must yield to an older, stronger, more experienced flock member at foraging places, roosting spots, and nesting sites.

A pet Eclectus instinctively uses this ability to determine its owner's mood. For instance, you, the owner, might notice some interesting activity at the wild bird feeder just outside the kitchen window. You know that your parrot loves to watch the wild birds, so you hurry into the next room to get him out of his cage. Your Eclectus senses immediately that your energy level has skyrocketed, but he is not sure why. His adrenaline level soars as he tries to determine if you are angry, in danger, or have suddenly decided to repossess the blueberries that you gave him for breakfast. When you open the cage door to reach for him, his head lowers, his eyes flash, and the hackles on his back and neck rise as he warns you that he is prepared to defend himself, his food, and his territory. The person who ignores or misinterprets the bird's body language is likely to receive a bite—and it wasn't the parrot's fault!

Be aware of your energy level when you handle your Eclectus. Don't work with your bird if you are stressed, nervous, upset, or angry. The parrot will sense it and respond accordingly. If your Eclectus is eating, preening, or sleeping, it will probably object to being disturbed.

Always talk to your parrot and explain in advance what you are going to do. Control is necessary, but be reasonable about your requests and respect your parrot's feelings.

Understanding and Guiding Eclectus Behaviors

Why Parrots Bite

Wild parrots rarely bite other parrots because they are able to convey their feelings through vocalization and body language, and can easily avoid confrontations by flying away. A caged bird with clipped wings doesn't have that option and may bite when it is frightened, confused, or feels cornered. The bird soon learns that it can control any situation with aggression and the result is a parrot that is no longer a welcome member of its family.

"Beaking": Parrot beaks and tongues are the highly sensitive equivalent of human fingertips. They are used for social interaction, touching, exploring, and eating. Playful "beaking" is a natural way for your Eclectus to interact with you, but you must be consistent about making the bird understand how much pressure you will allow. Parrots are empathic creatures that are acutely aware of our body language and facial expressions. They quickly learn that we smile when we are pleased and frown when we are unhappy. If the bird pinches harder than you feel is necessary, say *"No"* quietly but firmly and give it an extremely stern look. Keep a small favorite toy handy to distract the bird when it gets too rough.

Another way of communicating the no-biting rule to your parrot is a training method

TIP

Shoulders

Most behaviorists strongly urge parrot owners not to allow their birds on their shoulders. Having a parrot so close to your eyes is asking for trouble, especially since people often have difficulty understanding when or why their bird might bite.

sometimes referred to as an "earthquake." Hold the Eclectus on your hand or arm close to your body. When the bird bites, jerk your arm quickly and sharply downward an inch or two to startle

An Eclectus hen exhibiting extreme anger. Note the raised feathers and flashing eyes. This bird should be allowed plenty of time to calm down before any attempt is made to handle her.

it and put it slightly off balance, but remember, *the bird should never be allowed to fall.*

Overstimulation: An Eclectus may become overstimulated while tussling happily with its toys. The play becomes aggressive as the bird's excitement escalates and it begins squealing, growling, and shaking the toy as if it were an imaginary intruder. No harm is done unless the owner ignores the bird's body language and decides that this would be a good time to play with it. The bird is likely to bite because it is temporarily out of control, *not* because it is vicious or aggressive. The owner must wait for the bird's energy level to return to normal before attempting any interaction.

Territorial behavior: A shortage of suitable nesting sites often limits wild parrots' efforts to raise a family, so it is natural for them to defend their perceived territory with a great deal of determination. Parrots often seem to equate height with dominance, especially in the vicinity of their cages. A young adult Eclectus attempting to test your authority may become stubborn and nippy when you try to remove it from its high cage top. This territorial behavior can be tempered by teaching the bird to stay on a separate play gym when it is

This Eclectus hen is defending her nest against an intruder. If necessary, she will bite hard and hang on tightly. Pet Eclectus sometimes exhibit territorial behavior in and around their cages.

Portable playstands and play gyms allow a pet Eclectus to be included in family activities.

out of its cage. Ideally, this play area would be portable (or there would be more than one) so it could be moved wherever you happen to be. Owners miss much of the fun of having an Eclectus when they don't make this effort! If there is food, water, and toys to play with on the stand, it will not be difficult, with a little patience and persistence to teach the bird to stay put. The bird must be watched closely at first so that it can be quickly and gently returned to the playstand each time it climbs down, using the *"Up"* and *"Down"* commands discussed previously. If it persists, return it to its cage for five minutes each time it gets off the stand. A "time out" should never be longer than five minutes or the bird will not connect it with doing something wrong. Praise the bird often in an enthusiastic manner while it is on the stand.

Displacement biting: Displacement biting is a form of redirected aggression that can be extremely puzzling and upsetting to a bird's owner. It happens most often in mature parrots or those that are approaching sexual maturity. The owner is holding the bird when a person or household pet that it either dislikes or of whom it is jealous enters the room. The bird cannot reach the other person or animal so it bites its owner instead.

This Solomon Islands male's favorite place to play is on top of his owner's kitchen cupboards. He doesn't chew the woodwork and, unlike some Eclectus parrots, rarely displays height-related dominant behavior.

Fear behaviors: A bird that is poked at or teased by children will develop fear behaviors such as screaming and defensive biting. Even aggressive acts from a distance, such as pointing

TIP

Why Punishment Doesn't Work

It is often said that trust is the basis of all successful relationships, and it is especially true when working with your Eclectus. Losing your temper, squirting the bird in the face, yelling, dropping, or hitting the bird or its cage, or putting it in a dark room may temporarily stop unwanted behavior, but will also prevent you from ever achieving a close, trusting relationship with your Eclectus.

According to author and avian behaviorist Bonnie Munro Doane, "Because the bird has no evolutionary experience of violence as the reward of inappropriate behavior, it does not understand punishment intellectually in terms of cause and effect. Punishment therefore is seen as life-threatening, and the bird acts to protect itself rather than to change a behavior seen by its humans as 'bad'." An immediate, nonaggressive reaction works much better than complex punishment. A quiet but firm "No" and a stern look, then putting the bird down or quickly leaving the room will convey your feelings in a way the bird can readily understand.

Never underestimate the effectiveness of praise when working with a parrot. So often, owners ignore good behavior and effectively reinforce bad behavior by giving the parrot the attention it craves only when it misbehaves.

a stick and yelling *"Bang!"* cause distress. Some birds are afraid of baseball caps while others are uneasy around certain bright colors. Try to be as aware of your Eclectus' body language as it is of yours so that you will know when it is unhappy about something.

Don't put yourself in the position of being bitten. If your bird is overstimulated, territorial, or just having a bad day, leave it alone. A bath will often coax a grumpy bird into a mellow mood.

Whatever your Eclectus' reason for biting, don't overreact, don't punish the bird, and, above all, don't take it personally! The best way to respond to a bite (or any other negative behavior) is to ignore it as best you can and then *try to figure out why it happened.*

Why Parrots Scream

Parrots are highly social animals and communicating with other flock members while maneuvering through the vast forest canopy requires awesome vocal abilities. While Eclectus can be *very* loud at times, their vocalizations are generally brief and to the point, rarely for the sheer joy of making noise. An Eclectus that screams for long periods is telling you that it is unhappy about something.

Contact calls: Young Eclectus know instinctively that survival depends on their ability to keep up with the flock and they sometimes scream from separation anxiety when their owner leaves the room. The owner can help the bird through this difficult period by using *contact calls* to communicate with it when he or she has to leave the room. Saying things like *"You're OK"* and *"I'll be back soon"* reassure the youngster when it calls out—exactly as its wild flock would. Sally Blanchard states that "Constantly returning and initiating contact calls is one of the best ways to prevent screaming in young parrots and is also a positive way to work with established screaming behavior."

Environmental stimulation: Too much environmental stimulation can lead to nervousness, screaming, aggression, or refusal to leave its cage because the bird is not able to move to a quieter, safer location. All parrots need to feel part of their family or flock, but it will depend on the personality of the bird and the family's size and chaos level as to whether it would prefer to observe activities from a safe distance or be in the midst of it all. An Eclectus needs at least ten hours of uninterrupted sleep each night. Covering the cage at night may help, but if it is located in a well-lit, high-traffic area, if the television is nearby, and if there are family members on different schedules, your Eclectus will probably be happier with a small (24 inch × 24 inch [61 × 61 cm]) sleeping cage in a quiet room. The author knows an Eclectus that climbs down from her cage or playstand at a certain time each night, climbs the stairs, and puts herself to bed in her sleeping cage.

Daily routine: A daily routine is often touted as being necessary to the well-being of pet parrots. This idea had merit back when parrots were still being imported and a set routine was important for nervous wild-caught birds that doubtless felt a certain security in knowing exactly what to expect. However, birds kept on rigid schedules become rigid in their expectations and tend to suffer stress when they experience change of any kind. Domestic pet parrots are far more flexible, and, *providing they are happy and well cared for,* adjust easily to the changes in our daily lives. One should keep in mind though, that food is extremely important to an Eclectus and late meals will make it grumpy. Be sure that you stock your bird's cage with plenty of its favorite foods if you plan to be away longer than usual.

Chewing

Chewing is natural for all parrots and should never be considered misbehaving. There should be plenty of soft wood, rope, leather, and paper toys in the bird's cage and play areas to encourage chewing and shredding, and it is the owner's responsibility to supervise their Eclectus when it is in other parts of the house. A parrot that has been trained to remain on a portable play area when it is away from its cage is less likely to get into mischief.

Sexual Behavior in Pet Eclectus

Depending on the subspecies, Eclectus generally reach sexual maturity between the ages of two and four years. It is normal for raging hormones to cause a pet bird to attempt to form a more intense relationship with its favorite person. A male Eclectus may regurgitate food for a loved one exactly as he would for a mate. The owner should consider this a compliment, never a reason for punishment. The bird should be gently returned to his cage or play area or distracted with a favorite toy. Stroking a mature Eclectus on the back or under the tail could inadvertently stimulate breeding instincts. A male bird may attempt to mate with a hand or arm and a female might look for a dark corner suitable for nesting. This does not mean that the bird needs a mate of its own kind. An Eclectus that has bonded closely with humans all of its life is seldom able to transfer its affection to another bird and would be truly unhappy if forced into a breeding situation.

BREEDING ECLECTUS PARROTS

Breeding Eclectus parrots can be an enjoyable, rewarding hobby, but it is not an endeavor for the person in a hurry. A great deal of time and care is necessary to raise healthy, well-socialized baby parrots.

The Challenge

People often ask how breeding parrots as a hobby differs from breeding domestic animals such as dogs and cats. Perhaps the most challenging aspect for the breeder is that the pair of birds must be compatible. They must support each other through the hard work of nest preparation, incubation, protecting the eggs and chicks, and procuring food for their growing family. An Eclectus hen cannot do this by herself as a female mammal might. Wild Eclectus choose their mates through an elaborate courtship process that goes a long way toward assuring future compatibility. Locating a suitable mate for an adult bird is never a certainty and serious problems including aggression and infertility may arise when birds are forced to accept mates of the breeder's choosing. Large breeders solve this problem by allowing several baby Eclectus to grow up together and pair off

A Solomon Islands Eclectus hen guards the entrance of her nest box. Even in the wild, breeding females rarely venture far from their nests.

naturally. As previously discussed, a pet Eclectus that has not had close contact with its own kind throughout its life is usually too imprinted upon humans to make the transition to a breeding bird.

A major problem facing today's Eclectus breeder is finding a source of pure breeding stock. Of the five subspecies available in the United States, only the females can be identified by appearance. The males are so similar that without knowing the bird's history, even the experts can be fooled. Over the years this has led to a great deal of crossbreeding, or *hybridizing*, by careless and unscrupulous breeders. There is concern within the avicultural community that if such practices continue, the beautiful Eclectus subspecies with their subtle variations in appearance, habits, and vocalizations will disappear forever.

Once the budding aviculturist has obtained a compatible pair of birds of the same subspecies, more challenges lie ahead. It can take months (sometimes years!) for a male Eclectus to learn to copulate successfully and to feed his mate. Most females eventually become excellent mothers, but some consistently require assistance with incubating eggs or feeding chicks. A person intent on financial gain rarely lasts long, but for the dedicated hobbyist with an abundance of patience and love for the species, the reward is a healthy baby Eclectus that they helped bring into the world.

Obtaining Birds for Breeding

There are several options for the person who wants to obtain a pair of Eclectus for breeding. The first, and in the author's opinion, the best, is to buy two healthy unrelated babies *of the same subspecies* and raise them together. Solomon Islands youngsters are sexually mature in about two years, while the larger subspecies will take three to four years. The best thing about starting with young birds is that they are likely to remain gentle and trusting with their owner even while raising chicks of their own. The second possibility is to purchase a proven pair of birds. While the proven pair might seem the logical choice, a great deal depends on the honesty of the seller. Unless he or she is parting with all of his or her breeding stock, the buyer is justified in wondering why the seller would sell these particular birds. The seller should be willing to make available all of the pair's records detailing origin, age, health, and breeding history. Mature birds are much more likely to be stressed by being uprooted and could take many months to resume breeding. If you plan to introduce two adult birds from different sources, it will be necessary to house them side by side in separate cages until the time they begin to show an interest in each other. Breeding parrots is not an endeavor for the person in a hurry!

Setting Up a Pair of Eclectus for Breeding

Room: Whether you are breeding your Eclectus indoors or outdoors, it is important for their health and compatibility to give them plenty of room. A pair may appear to get along, but if a male is stressed by occasionally being unable to put enough space between himself and his more aggressive mate, his lack of confidence will likely result in infertile eggs. A suspended or walk-in breeding cage or *flight* 3 or 4 feet (91–122 cm) wide, at least 4 feet (122 cm) high, and 6 to 10 feet (183–305 cm) long will encourage flying and keep the birds happy and in good condition. Breeding birds will exhibit more confidence when their perches and nest box entrance are above human eye level. While territorial behavior toward people should be discouraged in pet Eclectus, it often serves to strengthen the pair bond in breeding birds. It is not unusual, though, for some pairs to remain gentle and affectionate toward their owner even while incubating eggs and feeding youngsters.

Perches: Perches should be of textured or roughened natural wood and should be fastened securely so that they don't slip or turn. A male Eclectus must balance precariously on the back of the female while mating, and wobbly perches are a common cause of infertile eggs. It is important for breeding birds to have toys to play with and fresh green branches to chew.

Nest Boxes

Eclectus generally aren't particular about the type of nest box they use. The vertical grandfather clock style is easiest to construct and works well if the hen isn't prone to jumping on her eggs. It requires a secure ladder or rungs for climbing in and out. Dimensions should be about 12 inches (30 cm) square by 24 to 36 inches (61–91 cm) high, with a 4 inch (10 cm) entrance hole in the upper third of the box and an inspection door about 4 inches from the bottom. Be sure the inspection opening is large enough for your hand and a chubby baby Eclectus!

"Z" boxes have been popular for Eclectus for many years and are highly recommended though they are more difficult to build and more costly to buy. The gently sloping ramp keeps the hen from jumping or falling on her eggs.

While the style of box isn't important, the author prefers wooden boxes to metal ones. Allowing the male to help with nest preparation by chewing and enlarging the entrance and excavating the interior as he would in the wild strengthens the pair bond and stimulates breeding. Strips of soft pine 2 × 2s or 2 × 4s can be fastened to the inside of the box near the bottom so the hen has something to chew. Wood boxes are also warmer in winter and cooler in summer. Breeders who prefer metal nest boxes could fasten wood near the entrance and in the bottom of the box to satisfy the birds' need to remodel. White pine or aspen shavings work well as nesting material, but avoid fine sawdust that might cause respiratory problems. Cedar shavings should not be used in a confined area such as a nest box or pet carrier.

Nesting Behavior

Once a hen goes into breeding mode, she spends nearly all of the time in her nest box. It is important that the two birds have formed a strong pair bond, evidenced by mutual feeding, before you give them a box; otherwise, the hen is quite likely to produce infertile eggs as she carries on happily with her nesting duties without help from the male. Another pair of Eclectus nearby will often stimulate courtship behavior in an overly timid male; however, loud, active parrots of other species may distract Eclectus to the point that they refuse to breed.

Incubation

When the hen begins to solicit mating by the male, the first egg generally follows within a couple of weeks. The hen lays two (occasionally three) eggs with two days between eggs. She usually keeps the male out of the box after the eggs are laid, although he continues to feed her and remains protective of their territory and acutely interested in everything she does. Incubation lasts about 28 days. The eggs can be candled after a week or so with a small flashlight or candling lamp while the hen is away from the box. A growing embryo will look like a dark red dot surrounded by thin blood vessels. If the eggs are clear—as they often are in the beginning—they should be left for the full incubation time. This will prevent the hen from depleting her calcium reserves by laying clutches too close together. Don't handle the eggs or disturb the pair more than absolutely necessary.

As the eggs near their hatch date, the hen sometimes makes squeaky begging noises that seem to encourage the male to feed her more often. The male's excitement will be obvious as he stands guard near the entrance, waiting for a peek at a newly hatched baby. He is likely to screech a loud warning if someone he doesn't approve of approaches the box.

Mutual feeding between a male and female Eclectus is a good indication of compatibility.

The male Eclectus feeds his mate with regurgitated food at the entrance to the nest while she is incubating eggs and caring for chicks.

An Eclectus hen indicates her breeding receptiveness by raising her head, lowering her body, and backing slowly toward the male. Copulation occurs with the male balancing precariously on the hen's back.

Two, occasionally three, eggs are a normal clutch for Eclectus parrots. Dust-free white pine or aspen shavings are suitable nesting materials.

It is important to disturb an Eclectus hen as little as possible while she is caring for eggs and chicks.

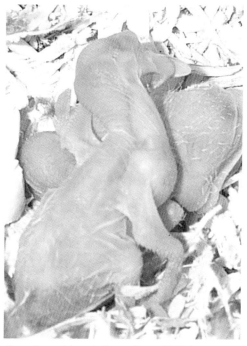

A "Z" style nest box with the inspection door raised. The sloped ramp leading to the nesting chamber lessens the possibility of the hen accidentally falling on and breaking her eggs.

One-day-old and three-day-old Eclectus chicks.

Caring for the Chicks

The chicks hatch 24 to 72 hours after the first *pip*, or piercing of the shell, usually 24 to 36 hours apart. An Eclectus baby is born with a food reserve in the form of a yolk sac in its abdomen that is slowly absorbed. It may be 24 hours before it is hungry enough to solicit feeding from the hen, so it is important not to assume too quickly that she isn't doing her job. A tiny bubble of liquid in the chick's crop indicates that it is being fed. It is wise to leave a young hen alone during this critical period. Her instincts will lead her if she is not distracted by well-intentioned nest box inspections, and there is no doubt that parrots learn from experience.

Eclectus chicks are born blind and naked and should be reared by the hen if they are to receive the best possible start in life. Unless she stops feeding them earlier, they can be removed from the nest in three or four weeks, at which time they will need spoon or syringe feeding four or five times daily.

Hand-feeding

There are several good commercial hand-feeding formulas for parrots that need only mixing with warm water. The formula is fed at about 108°F (42°C). If it is too cold, the chick will refuse to eat; if it is too hot it will cause damage to delicate crop tissue. Microwave ovens should not be used because they create super-hot spots in the formula. Young chicks will readily swallow scalding hot food with no apparent discomfort, but the resulting burns are serious and always require veterinary attention. Chicks should normally be fed before their crops empty, although they should be allowed to empty completely once every 24 hours.

Care and patience is required when feeding baby Eclectus because their feeding response is weak and they refuse to be rushed. The feeding response is a parrot chick's rapid thrusting and bobbing head movements indicating that its glottis or windpipe entrance is closed and it can safely swallow food. A weak response makes the possibility of aspiration, or introducing food into the windpipe, much greater. A spoon with the sides bent up seems to elicit a stronger response than a syringe, perhaps because the shape and feel are similar to the hen's beak.

Possible Problems

Only with experience does one learn to recognize the many things that can go wrong before it is too late to save the chick. A hand-feeder must know immediately if a baby is too warm or too cold, if its skin is too dry, if it is dehydrated, if its crop is emptying too quickly or too slowly, or if the weight gain made in the last 24 hours was sufficient. It is important to maintain a clean, stress-free environment because young Eclectus have poorly developed immune systems and are susceptible to bacterial infections.

Constricted Toe Syndrome: The breeder should be watchful for a condition known as Constricted Toe Syndrome that is common in very young Eclectus chicks. It appears exactly as if a thin piece of thread has become wound tightly around the chick's toe causing a constriction of the digit. It is not considered life threatening but if not noticed soon enough, the end of the toe will turn pale, dry up, and slough off. Increasing the brooder humidity and providing moist hot compresses and massage in the early stages may soften the lesion, which may eventually disappear. In most cases however, surgery is necessary to remove the constricting tissue fibers. The cause is unknown but has been linked to low brooder humidity and staphylococcus bacteria.

Temperature

If the hen shows no interest in feeding her chicks, the breeder will have to assume responsibility for their care. Day-old Eclectus chicks need feeding every two hours and should be kept at a temperature of 98.5°F (36.9°C) for the first couple of days. A thermostatically controlled brooder will be necessary for the helpless, naked chicks that cannot control their body heat or easily move toward or away from a heat source. The temperature can be slowly lowered to about 94°F (34.4°C) by the end of the first week and very gradually thereafter. Watch the chicks closely because behavior is a better indicator of their comfort than a thermometer reading. If they are hot they will be restless and breathe heavily. Cold babies will huddle together, be lethargic, and may refuse to eat. A chick's wingtip should feel warm between your lips.

Very young babies should be housed in the brooder in small plastic containers lined with cotton washcloths. Paper toweling and tissues do not provide secure footing and can result in *splayed legs,* a common deformity that results when a chick cannot keep its feet directly under its body. Babies always do best if they are kept together.

Independence

At three or four weeks an Eclectus chick is covered with dark woolly down. Very soon it will be possible to detect a faint shimmer of color as the emerging pinfeathers indicate whether it is male or female. Eclectus babies possess a quiet awareness at a very young age and should always be spoken to and handled with gentleness. They generally *wean* or no longer require hand-feeding at three or four months, but each bird is different and should be allowed to become independent at its own pace. You can begin offering cooked and fresh soft foods, shelled almonds, and millet spray in easily accessible dishes at about six weeks. This is a good time to accustom baby Eclectus to gentle petting and touching so it will enjoy being handled throughout its life.

This chapter is meant only to give the reader an idea of the effort and knowledge required to successfully breed and raise Eclectus parrots. It is strongly recommended that you join a local bird club, read current publications, and attend any of the national organizations of aviculturists that sponsor educational conferences and lectures by breeders and veterinarians (see Information, page 92, for addresses).

ECLECTUS IN THE WILD

Due to rapid deforestation and destruction of their natural habitat, the future of several subspecies of Eclectus parrots is in doubt. It is important that the existence of pure subspecies remaining in captivity is not jeopardized by careless hybridizing.

Natural Behavior

Range: The natural range of Eclectus parrots includes New Guinea, the Solomon Islands, the Islands of Indonesia, and the Cape York Peninsula of Australia. Their habitat is the canopy of densely wooded semitropical to tropical rain forests. Nest sites are usually in deep hollows of standing trees near the edge of the forest or in a clearing, and there have been reports of more than one pair nesting in the same tree. Nesting in the wild has been reported almost year-round.

Flocks of males are commonly seen squabbling noisily over choice food and roosting sites. When females are sighted, their numbers are generally much smaller and they tend to be less raucous and conspicuous. It is suspected that mature females spend most of the time

A pair of Vosmaeri Eclectus (E. roratus vosmaeri) from the northern and central Moluccan Islands.

in and around their nests, either caring for eggs and chicks or perhaps protecting the site from being appropriated by other hens.

Food: Eclectus are arboreal, which means that their natural food consists of nuts, seeds, fruit, buds, shoots, and blossoms found high in the treetops. They also raid plantings of grain, corn, bananas, coconut, and papaya, and are considered serious pests by native villagers.

Courtship: When a pair is courting, the male approaches the female and feeds her. He then taps his beak sharply on the perch and leans from side to side, quickly touching each side of the hen's head with his head and neck. The hen chases the male and begs to be fed prior to allowing him to mount her for mating. The hen lays two, occasionally three white eggs on a layer of chewed wood chips. She sits tightly for approximately 28 days, leaving the nest only when the male returns to feed her.

Cooperative breeding: Small groups of males have been observed attending the same nesting hens. It is thought that this may be a simple form of cooperative breeding common to some species of birds whereby youngsters from the previous year help the parents raise their younger siblings. This would explain why many young domestic male Eclectus are slow to learn that they must supply food to their mate and chicks. Breeders are finding that many species of parrots are seriously handicapped in their ability to communicate with a mate if they do not grow up in the company of others of their kind.

Note: Two Eclectus subspecies, *E. roratus riedeli* and *E. roratus cornelia* are seriously endangered in the wild. Most of the others will eventually be threatened by rapid deforestation and destruction of nesting sites.

Identifying the Subspecies

The genus *Eclectus* is composed of only one species, *roratus*, and approximately eight to ten subspecies or races.

The Males

The males of all the subspecies are similar. They are mainly green with the underwing coverts and the sides of the body bright red. The bend of the wing is bright blue and the outer webs of the primaries are a darker blue. The outer tail feathers are suffused with blue. The underside of the tail is gray-black, tipped with yellow. The upper mandible is orange, tipped with paler yellow. The iris is orange. Males of the various subspecies exhibit subtle differences in size, in the shade of green, and in the amount of yellow and blue in the tail, but without knowing a male's origin, it is impossible to ascertain its race.

The Females

Descriptions of the females of the Eclectus subspecies commonly available in the United States are as follows

✔ Red-sided Eclectus *(E. roratus polychloros)* from New Guinea and the western Papuan Islands. More stocky appearance than Vosmaeri. Definite line of separation between the red head and neck and the royal blue of the lower breast and abdomen. Blue eye ring. Back and upper wing coverts are maroon. Tail is maroon with a 1-inch (2.5 cm) red band at the end. Creamy white eyes as adults.

✔ Aru Red-sided *(E. roratus aruensis)* are found only on the islands of Aru. Differs only slightly from the Red-sided in that it is larger, weighing up to 600 grams.

✔ Solomon Islands Eclectus *(E. roratus solomonesis)* from the Solomon Islands, Admiralty Islands, and Bismarck Archipelago. The smallest Eclectus weighs 350–425 grams. Same as Red-sided except smaller and more compact with shorter neck and tail. Wing tips extend only to tip of tail. Head is rounder. Blue eye ring is generally more distinct than in Red-sided. Creamy white eyes as adults.

✔ Vosmaeri Eclectus (*E. roratus vosmaeri*) from the northern and central Moluccan Islands. Appears longer and slimmer than Red-sided. No definite line of separation between head and breast colors. No blue eye ring. Belly is deep lavender or mauve. Back and upper wing coverts are a bright, dark red. Tail has a 1- to 2½-inch (2.5–6.6 cm) band of pure golden-yellow at the end. Yellow V-shaped undertail coverts. Golden-yellow eyes.

✔ Grand Eclectus (*E. roratus roratus*) from the southern Moluccan Islands. The nominate of the genus. Definite line of separation between the red head and neck and the deep, dark purple of the breast and abdomen. Undertail coverts are orange-red. No blue eye ring. Tail band is a muted orange-red tipped with a thin edging of dusty yellow. Upper wing coverts and back are dark maroon. Golden-yellow eyes.

The following Eclectus subspecies are considered extremely rare in the United States:

✔ *E. r. macgillivrayi,* from the Cape York Peninsula of Australia. Largest of all subspecies at 14½ inches (37 cm). Identical to the Red-sided but larger. Rare in the United States.

✔ Biaki *(Eclectus roratus biaki)* from the island of Biak. Like the Red-sided but smaller with somewhat brighter head, neck, and bib. Rare in the United States.

✔ *E. roratus riedeli* from the Tanimbar Islands. Solid red with no trace of blue, purple, or lavender. Yellow undertail coverts and broad yellow tail band. Rare in the United States and seriously endangered in the wild.

✔ Cornelia's Eclectus *(E. roratus cornelia)* from the island of Sumba. Solid bright red on head and breast with no trace of blue, purple, or lavender. Back is a lighter maroon than in other subspecies. Tail tipped in yellow. Rare in the United States and seriously endangered in the wild.

Dealing with Hybrids

No one knows for certain how many thousands of years it took each isolated subspecies of Eclectus parrot to evolve after separating from the original population, but it is important that we recognize how precious, unique, and irreplaceable each one is. At least two subspecies are seriously threatened by deforestation and it is likely that others will become endangered in the future. Importation bans have eliminated the possibility of increasing the gene pool in this country, and unless concerned aviculturists and breeders take responsibility for keeping our captive breeding stock pure, there is a real danger that these pure subspecies will eventually be replaced by hybrids.

According to Eclectus breeder and author Laurella Desborough the problem with hybrids is more than just losing color patterns. Each subspecies has its own vocalizations, behaviors, and developmental time lines that disappear with crossbreeding. Because males of the various subspecies are similar, many breeders are unaware that they are mixing Eclectus subspecies until it becomes evident from the appearance of the young females they produce. Others simply don't care because hybrids are readily accepted in the pet trade. It is obvious that there are a large number of crossbred birds in this country, both in breeding situations and as pets, and the problem is likely to worsen with time.

Hybrid Eclectus may or may not resemble one of the pure subspecies. Some have partial blue eye rings; others have narrow yellow tail bands or a combination of blue eye rings and yellow tail bands. Young females that show different color patterns than their mothers or sisters are good indicators of mixed parentage.

Hybrids make good pets and are often utilized as foster parents for pure Eclectus subspecies and other species of parrots with less than perfect parenting abilities. Desborough suggests that breeders identify crossbred Eclectus by including an X in their band numbers to help prevent them from being mistakenly purchased for breeding.

These male Eclectus are playing in a lilac tree. The natural habitat of Eclectus parrots is high in the dense canopy of the rain forest.

Three Solomon Islands Eclectus females. This slightly smaller subspecies tends to be gentle and easygoing.

*Left: Tail of a Vosmaeri
Eclectus female. Note the
wide band of pure yellow.*

*Middle: Tail of a Grand
Eclectus female. Note the red-
orange band tipped with a
thin edging of dusty yellow.*

*Right: The tail of a Red-sided
Eclectus female is maroon
with a 1-inch red band at the
end. The tail of a Solomon
Islands female is similar to
the Red-sided except that it is
shorter, extending barely past
the wing tips.*

*A male Eclectus often is
not allowed inside the
nest box. His job is to
stand guard and warn his
mate of possible danger.*

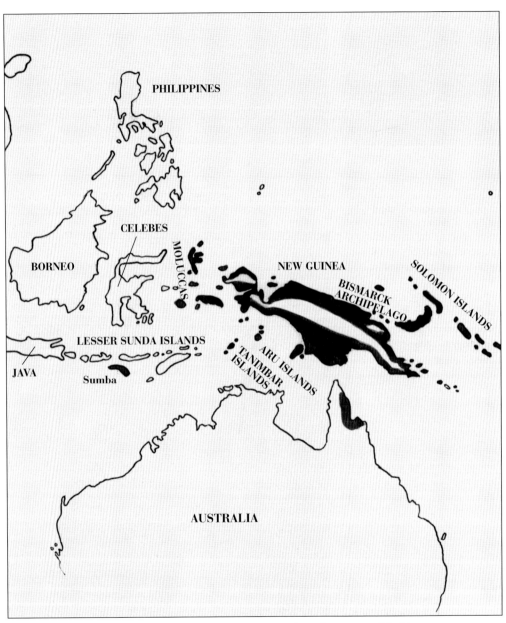

Range map for Eclectus parrots. The darkened areas show their natural habitat.

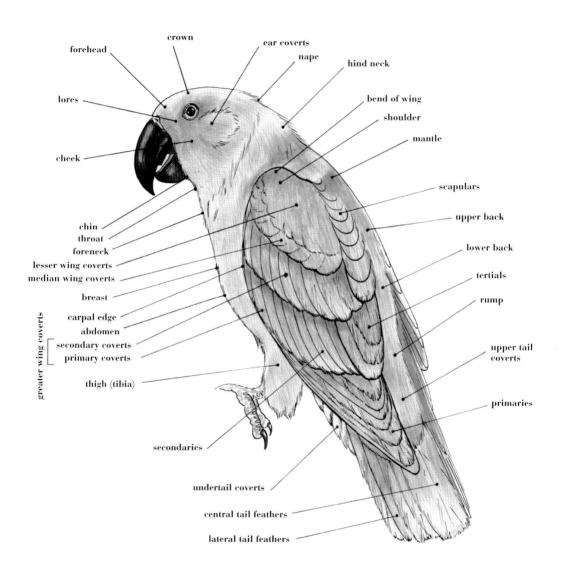

crown

ear coverts

forehead

nape

hind neck

lores

bend of wing

shoulder

mantle

cheek

scapulars

upper back

chin
throat
foreneck
lesser wing coverts
median wing coverts

lower back

tertials

breast

rump

greater wing coverts

carpal edge
abdomen
secondary coverts
primary coverts

upper tail
coverts

thigh (tibia)

primaries

secondaries

undertail coverts

central tail feathers

lateral tail feathers

The parts of an Eclectus parrot.

INFORMATION

Organizations

American Federation of Aviculture (AFA)
3118 West Thomas Road, #713
Phoenix, AZ 85079-6218

Midwest Avian Research Expo (MARE)
12117 Wright Road
Berlin Heights, OH 44814

Association of Avian Veterinarians (AAV)
P.O. Box 811720
Boca Raton, FL 33481
Phone: (561) 393-8901

World Parrot Trust USA
P.O. Box 341141
Memphis, TN 38184
Phone: (901) 873-3616

Mail Order Parrot Supplies

Hornbeck's
7088 Lyndon Street
Rosemont, IL 60018
Phone: (888) 224-3247
Web site: *www.hornbecks.com*

Magazines

The AFA Watchbird
P.O. Box 56218
Phoenix, AZ 85079-6218
Phone: (602) 484-0931

Bird Talk
P.O. Box 57347
Boulder, CO 80322-7347
Phone: (800) 365-4421

Companion Parrot Quarterly
(formerly *The Pet Bird Report*)
P.O. Box 2428
Alameda, CA 94501
Phone: (510) 523-5303
Web site: *www.companionparrot.com*

Parrots
Imax Publishing Ltd.
Unit B2, Dolphin Way
Shoreham-By-Sea
West Sussex BN43 6NZ England
Phone: 01273 464777
Web site: *www.parrotmag.com*

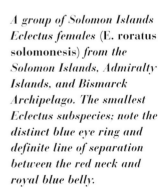

A group of Solomon Islands Eclectus females (E. roratus solomonesis) from the Solomon Islands, Admiralty Islands, and Bismarck Archipelago. The smallest Eclectus subspecies: note the distinct blue eye ring and definite line of separation between the red neck and royal blue belly.

GLOSSARY

Aspiration when food enters the airways of a young parrot; common with gavage or tube-feeding and with inexperienced hand-feeders.

Aviculture keeping and breeding birds in captivity.

Blood feather new, growing feather, usually in the wing or tail, that is still connected to its blood supply.

Clutch number of eggs laid and cared for by a hen during one nesting period.

Contact calls vocalizations between birds in a flock that help them stay in touch.

Copulation sexual intercourse between two birds.

Crop pouchlike storage area in the esophagus that holds food prior to digestion.

Domestic describing parrots that have been bred and raised in captivity.

Fledge to fly for the first time.

Full-spectrum lighting artificial lighting that contains the full spectrum of colors found in natural sunlight.

Gavage or tube-feeding feeding chicks by inserting a tube directly into their crops. Babies fed in this manner are at risk of injury and aspiration and often have difficulty learning to eat by themselves.

Hybridizing mating birds of different sub-species together.

Mandible the upper or lower part of a bird's beak.

Primary feathers first ten flight feathers on a parrot's wing.

Proventriculus stomach.

Regurgitation bringing up partially digested food from the crop or stomach to feed a mate or chicks.

Sexual dimorphism difference in appearance between males and females of the same species.

Socialization teaching baby parrots how to get along in the human environment.

Ventriculus gizzard, where food is ground up during the digestive process.

Original Flying Machine
10645 N. Tatum Boulevard
Suite 200 #459
Phoenix, AZ 85028-3053
Phone: (877) OFM-BIRD

Books

Athan, Mattie Sue. *Guide to a Well-Behaved Parrot.* Hauppauge, NY: Barron's Educational Series, Inc., 1993.

Blanchard, S., *Companion Parrot Handbook.* Alameda, CA: Pet Bird Information Council, Inc., 1999.

Doane, Bonnie Munro. *My Parrot, My Friend.* New York: Howell Book House, 1994.

___. *The Parrot in Health and Illness.* New York: Howell Book House, 1991.

Web Sites

Land of Vos
www.landofvos.com

About the Author

Katy McElroy saw her first wild parrot while living in Australia 30 years ago, and has been keeping and breeding them ever since. She is particularly interested in their natural behavior in the wild, and how this knowledge can enable us to better understand and manage our pets and breeding birds. She owns and operates a commercial aviary, is the author of many articles on parrot behavior, and is a frequent speaker on the advantages of outdoor breeding flights and nest box surveillance cameras to increase our understanding of the relationships between parent birds and their offspring.

Cover Photos

B. Everett Webb

Photo Credits

Norvia Behling: pages 16 (top left) and 21 (top right); Susan Green: pages 20 (bottom right) and 29 (top left); Pieter van den Hooven: pages 28 (bottom right) and 41 (bottom); Katy McElroy: pages 8 (top and bottom), 9 (top and bottom), 17 (top and bottom), 28 (top and bottom left), 29 (right), 32, 36, 37, 40 (top), 41 (top), 44, 48 (top and bottom), 49 (top), 60, 61, 68, 72 (bottom), 73 (bottom), 76, 80 (top left, top right, middle left, middle right, and bottom), 81 (top left, top right, and bottom left), and (89 bottom); Dean Moser: pages 16 (top right, bottom left, and bottom right), 20 (left), 49 (bottom), 56, 72 (top), 73 (top), 81 (bottom right), and 88 (top); B. Everett Webb: pages 2–3, 4, 5, 12, 13, 20 (top right), 21 (top left, bottom left, and bottom right), 24, 25, 29 (bottom left), 33, 45, 52, 53, 64, 65, 69, 77, 85, 88 (bottom), 89 (top left, top middle, top right), and 92.

Important Note

People who suffer from allergies to feathers or any kind of feather dust should not keep parrots. In case of doubt, check with a doctor before you acquire one.

In dealing with parrots, one may receive injuries from bites or scratches. Have such wounds attended to by a doctor. Although psittacosis (parrot fever) is not a common illness among parrots, it produces symptoms in both parrots and humans that may become life-threatening. At the first sign of a cold or flu, see a doctor.

Acknowledgments

The author would like to thank Lynn Devan for sharing her deep love and knowledge of Eclectus parrots, Dean Moser for the wonderful photographs of his birds and his family, and Gayle Soucek for her encouragement.

All inquiries should be addressed to:
Barron's Educational Series, Inc.
250 Wireless Boulevard
Hauppauge, NY 11788
http://www.barronseduc.com

Library of Congress Catalog Card No. 2001043188

ISBN-13: 978-0-7641-1886-9
ISBN-10: 0-7641-1886-2

Library of Congress Cataloging-in-Publication Data
McElroy, Katy.
   Eclectus parrots : everything about purchase, care, feeding, and housing / Katy McElroy.
     p. cm.
   Includes bibliographical references (p.).
   ISBN 0-7641-1886-2 (alk. paper)
   1. Parrots. I. Title.
SF473.P3 M36   2002
636.6'865—dc21   2001043188

Printed in China